MANAGING TIME

THE NO NONSENSE LIBRARY

NO NONSENSE CAREER GUIDES

Managing Time
How to Choose a Career
How to Re-enter the Workforce
How to Write a Resume
No Nonsense Interviewing
No Nonsense Management

NO NONSENSE FINANCIAL GUIDES

How to Use Credit and Credit Cards
Investing in Mutual Funds
Investing in the Stock Market
Investing in Tax Free Bonds
Understanding Money Market Funds
Understanding IRAs
Understanding Treasury Bills and Other U.S. Government Securities
Understanding Common Stocks
Understanding Stock Options and Futures Markets
Understanding Social Security
Understanding Insurance
How to Plan and Invest for Your Retirement
Making a Will and Creating Estate Plans

NO NONSENSE REAL ESTATE GUIDES

Understanding Condominiums and Co-ops
How to Buy a Home
Understanding Mortgages and Home Equity Loans

NO NONSENSE SUCCESS GUIDES

NO NONSENSE HEALTH GUIDES

NO NONSENSE COOKING GUIDES

NO NONSENSE PARENTING GUIDES

NO NONSENSE CAR GUIDES

NO NONSENSE CAREER GUIDE™

MANAGING TIME

ANDREW AMBRAZIEJUS

LONGMEADOW
PRESS

Cover design by Nancy Sabato
Interior design by Richard Oriolo

ISBN: 0-681-41404-9

Printed in United States of America

First Edition

0 9 8 7 6 5 4 3 2

CONTENTS

Introduction:
Why Manage Time?

"I'm behind in my work." "I have no time to do what really needs to be done." "If only the phone would stop ringing." "If only my secretary knew how to do this." "Where has the day gone?"

How often do we hear these statements from our friends and colleagues? And how often do we nod sympathetically, thinking about our own battles with time when we are at work? But then how often do we laugh and shrug it off, as if to agree that we're not happy with the current state of affairs either, but that there's nothing to be done?

The point of *Managing Time* is that something *can* be done about time pressures. It begins with an understanding that there are a certain number of fixed hours in the day. No more, no less. When we pay attention to time management, we learn to use those hours productively. We take an honest look at how we spend our day, so that we can't hide behind that favorite excuse, "I don't have time."

Think about how large a part of your life any job consumes. Every week you spend 40 or more hours at the workplace. Add time for commuting, preparing for work in the mornings, and unwinding from tension in the evenings—an hour each day, at least—that's another 10 hours for the week. Now subtract your hours of sleep, say about 50 or so, from a total of 168. What are you left with? Out of 118 waking hours, 45, 50, or 60 revolve around work. That's easily a third to a half of your life. And it doesn't include putting in late hours, an extra-long commute, working on weekends, or punching in at that second job. Anything that takes up so many of your hours deserves to be managed well.

For most of us, the work we do also provides a large measure of satisfaction in our lives. Whether we're merging companies or typing letters, we're happy when a job has been well done. The better we know how to use the hours devoted to whatever we're doing, the better we feel.

Finally, working in a *company* means we enter into a special relationship with many people—all working together, all trying to accomplish certain tasks. As the tasks and the people multiply, the demands on our time increase geometrically. Pressure builds and everything seems to rush by. It's easy to let things get out of control.

The cliché—that the world is moving faster and more seems to be required of us in a shorter amount of time—is all too true. Being able to respond adequately to the various demands placed on us so that we perform well under pressure and yet know where to draw the line is an important consideration for all us. Using time wisely is the primary tool in achieving this delicate balancing act.

PART ONE

—

WHAT IS TIME?

1

The Nature of Time: Respecting the Inevitable

What is time? *Webster's* defines it as "the measured or measurable period during which an action, process, or condition exists or continues." It is also "a continuum which lacks spatial dimensions and in which events succeed one another from past through present to future," and "the point or period when something occurs," or "a person's experience during a specified period or on a particular occasion." It all sounds rather abstract. Is there really not a more concrete way to define time?

Is it money, as the popular saying goes? Is it life itself, which some time management experts think is a good analogy? Or is focusing on experiences "during a specified period," as does *Webster's,* the best way to look at it?

We use the word *time* so often in our speech—complaining about it, praising it, or disparaging its effect on our lives—but do we really know what we mean by it? We say it has disappeared, but does time really disappear? Where does it go? Stopping to think these questions through will provide us with a framework for looking at time and seeing how it affects our lives, both inside the office and out. Having a better understanding of its nature is also a good way to start working with time and not against it, which is the ultimate goal of good time management.

You Cannot Manage Time— You Can Only Manage Yourself

Time is not manageable. Contrary to what the term time management implies, there is nothing you can do to make time change. You cannot really make it pass more slowly or go at a faster rate. You cannot stretch it. You cannot double it. You cannot make it stop. You can only manage your own behavior in relation to time.

Focusing on your own behavior is the first step in good time management. It forces you to prioritize and look at what you may be doing to make the passage of time seem frustrating. If you are rushing around, and there doesn't seem to be enough time to get things accomplished, you may *feel* that time is rushing by. But when you stop and examine the situation, you will realize that the time is not passing any more quickly than before. It only seems that way because you have either taken on too many tasks or your attention is being pulled in too many different directions. Unless you understand this and start making changes in your own behavior, time will never seem to work in your favor.

Let's say, for example, you are an office manager. You

pride yourself on doing things well, you have a lot of knowledge about the way things work, you are happy to share this information with the people in your office, and you derive a lot of satisfaction when everything runs smoothly. Suppose, however, business picks up. There seem to be more people who ask your advice, more problems that need to be resolved. Your day gets much busier and the time seems to pass by twice as fast as it did before. When you fall behind in your work you will be tempted to somehow blame time, asking "where has the day gone?" or making excuses such as "there's no time," or "the time flew by."

But if you are honest with yourself, you will have to admit that the passage of time has not changed, you have. Because of the increase in business, you have taken on more work as you try to deal with all those new people and resolve all those new problems. Your behavior is what has changed; time itself keeps passing as it always has.

Accepting the fact that any changes to improve the situation will have to be made in your own behavior is an important step. Suddenly you are in charge. And you don't have to do battle with time. All the energy you have spent being angry or frustrated can now go toward modifying your own behavior and recognizing how you try to keep up with the pace of things around you.

Time Does Not Stop

Over the years, many writers have used the image of a flowing river to describe time. Using a river is more than just poetic fancy, because it emphasizes the fact that time does not stand still. It is always moving along, the pace steady and unyielding. Time cannot be stopped or saved. When we talk about saving time, what we really mean is the adjustment of our behavior in a particular area; we stop doing certain things so that we can do others.

Thinking of time this way helps us better realize how easy it is to waste the time we do have. Once it's gone, it's gone, and the best we can do is to take the present moment and use it wisely. This won't make up for time wasted the day before: nothing can be done about the previous day. It is gone and today is the day that matters.

This is not to say, of course, that we must all run around trying to do everything, "grabbing all the gusto" we can, always worrying that time is passing by too quickly and that we'll never get enough of life. Being conscious of the movement of time means we respect it. We recognize that our time is not unlimited, so that we want to use the time we do have wisely. We begin to focus on "spending" time, not saving it.

The urgency created by the passage of time is hard to ignore. It exerts a strong influence on us; it's as if we want to behave the same way, not giving up a second of something so precious. We become suspicious of relaxing or stopping our activities in any way, feeling guilty that slowdown means wasted time. We get into the habit of living life in fits and starts—running around for a period of time, driving ourselves and everybody else to distraction, and then "crashing," stopping everything because our bodies and minds tell us they need time to recharge. So we rest for awhile, then pick ourselves up and go through the same rushing and stopping process again. On the job, this often manifests itself in working very hard on a particular project, perhaps letting all the routine tasks go, then crashing; feeling guilty, we get ourselves together, take care of the routine tasks that we have been ignoring, and then throw ourselves headlong into the next big project. Then we crash and feel guilty again, and on and on it goes.

The way out of this mode of behavior is learning to integrate different aspects of all of our activities. Certainly impossible deadlines are not all avoidable. Sometimes we have to throw ourselves wholeheartedly into a project, not leaving time for anything else. Unfortunately, it may be the only way keep on top of a job, not to mention get ahead. But if this becomes routine, a loud warning should be going off in your head. There is something wrong with the way you are managing yourself in relation to your time. The urgency about getting the most out of time has become chaos, your life is out of control. You must take your life back, acknowledging that the passage of time means living life in a fuller, not more hectic, manner.

You Have to Make Time— It Won't Be Created for You

It is up to us to find the time necessary to accomplish our goals—time won't magically manifest itself without our efforts. Accepting this fact means we take responsibility for what we do. The next time you want to say "I don't have the time" for something, tell yourself that what you are really saying is "I am not *making* the time." Practice this little exercise—the more you do it the more you will take responsibility for the choices you make in managing your time. You will see clearly how you are in charge, and how nothing will change until you do something about it.

The secret of making time is concentration. Consciously allowing yourself to focus on a particular activity is how you make time for it. Usually, this means you do not focus on anything else. It also means that, before starting, you think about how long this activity may take to do. The more accurately you can gauge this, the more confident you will be in allocating time for it and not worrying about all your other tasks—you always know that they will get their turn. This will come with experience, of course; if you make a habit of it, in fairly short order allocating time accurately will become second nature to you.

Not worrying about where your time is going helps in dealing with interruptions and those supposed emergencies too. When they happen, you are better able to keep focused and not shift your attention to a task that may not merit it.

Does concentrating on one activity at a time mean doing two things at once is impossible or is not considered good time management? Not necessarily. If you're making up the departmental budget or reviewing your assistant's performance, you will naturally exclude other activities because these tasks require your full attention. However, depending on how involved it is, that magazine article you've been waiting to read describing a certain aspect of your industry or those notes from a particular meeting which you've wanted to transcribe into more legible form can be done while you are on hold during a telephone call or are waiting outside someone's office while they finish with *their* telephone call.

Taking responsibility for finding the time to do things is also your prime weapon in combatting the "when/whenever" syndrome. "I'll do it whenever I have the time." "I'll reorganize my files when I get caught up." "I'll go speak to my boss about her rudeness when I feel more secure." "I'll tackle the boring tasks when I'm good and ready." Look closely at these statements. When you say you will do something "whenever" or "when," what you are really saying is that you do not want to do something *now*. However, you may find yourself putting off particular tasks until it is imperative that you do them or face dire consequences. Then you are forced to do something under pressure which could have been taken care of in a much more constructive way. By acknowledging that you have to make the time for something, you don't push it out of your mind, but make that extra effort not to let it slip away from you.

It Is Easier to Be Passive with Time than Active

We usually approach the activity that takes less energy before doing the one that requires more energy. Consider all the decisions you make when faced with various tasks. Don't you usually prefer to:

- do what you like before something you don't like
- do something that brings an immediate reward before something for which gratification is delayed
- do something simple before something that is complex
- do something routine before something never before attempted
- do something that will have an outcome of which you are fairly sure before something for which the outcome is less certain.

This need for instant gratification is a trait we all share, and it is never more apparent than when we look at our time priorities. The pull toward getting something done that will have a more obvious result more quickly achieved is overpowering. We all like accomplishing things—and the sooner the better. Never mind that when you think about it logically, it should be the other way around. Things that are more difficult, vague, unpleasant should be attempted first because they will require more energy and time. The simple, easier things will almost take care of themselves.

Understanding this need is important in any kind of planning that you may do. In theory, it seems perfectly fine to say you will spend that first hour of the morning on routine tasks such as looking through mail or returning yesterday's phone calls—and then you will sit down to write that report that's a week overdue. Or, you will take care of some mildly pressing but essentially pleasant matters before calling in that incompetent secretary of yours and finally firing him. The problem is, unless you're very careful, that first hour can easily stretch into two. If anything during that time of routine has served to upset you or create some tension, it will require that much more energy for you to get started on that report. If any of those mildly pressing matters become more pressing, you may easily decide that you cannot deal with your secretary today and you will put off firing him until tomorrow.

The problem with planning is that we usually forget to take into account that all-important entity—ourselves. Our stamina, moods, emotions, all influence our work. We all like to think of ourselves as professionals and pretend that they do not matter, but they do. What may seem on paper to be a good plan often falls apart because our energy level is just not where we would like it to be. We'll spend time doing what we like and what is easy, and when we come to what is difficult, there is not much left to give. Recognizing this tendency in ourselves vis-à-vis time can help you make better decisions in scheduling.

There Is Never Enough Time To Do Everything

How often do we make lists, decide that we will do a number of things during a certain period of time, and then when the time comes to actually do them we find that we only can finish a few? Wanting to do too much—if not everything!—seems to be a part of human nature. There is a lot that intrigues us, there is much that we in all good faith think we can accomplish as long as we put our minds to it. However, having respect for time includes recognizing the difference between trying hard to accomplish something and being unrealistic in the expectations that we put on ourselves.

When we take on these unreasonable expectations, time becomes an illusion. We think that time will somehow expand to encompass whatever we are doing. For example, if something takes two hours and we have an hour in which to do it, we often expect that the hour will somehow magically stretch into two and that we will still finish on time. We work in a rush, trying to compress what needs to be done into one hour. As unrealistic as such an expectation is, believing this gives us a feeling of power and control, and we fall for it again and again.

The truth of the matter is that it's the other way around: an activity expands to fill the time that has been allotted to it. This is known as Parkinson's law, named after a British professor who popularized the law in the 1950s. It is a variation on the infamous Murphy's Law, which states that if anything can go wrong it will. What these notions are saying is that although we think we're in control, it's time that is in charge, always being constant, and we are deluding ourselves if we think that we can shape it to our needs. When this truth comes up against all our wishes and plans for ourselves, we have to recognize time's constancy and adjust our lives to it. If we don't, we will constantly be running around, "trying to do too much," feeling both guilty and frustrated that time is not on our side. What started out as an attempt to be responsible becomes a frustrating experience of always playing catch-up. The sooner we realize that we will never be caught up with everything we want to do, the better off we will be.

2

You and Time:
Time Is Not the Enemy,
You Are

This is a chapter of questions you can ask yourself to see how
well you work with time. When going over them, you may
decide upon other questions that may be more pertinent to
you. More power to you! Time is a very personal thing; how
you use it ultimately depends upon your own needs and no one
else's.

The six questions in this chapter can be used as a way to
start a good time management program for yourself or to begin
to correct anything that has gone wrong. Whether you think
of yourself as one of the support staff, a supervisor, or a higher
level manager, take a look at these questions and respond to
them as honestly as you can.

1. How Do You Look at Time?

Do you view time as an enemy? Something that is passing by too quickly, something of which you never have enough, something that makes you crazy because it causes you to run around trying to get as much accomplished as possible? These views of time are commonplace. If it only weren't for time and its shortcomings, our lives would be much more sane and fulfilling—or so we believe.

We've already established that time does not "pass by" at different speeds—it is the events of our lives that make us feel that way. If we don't think we have enough time, we're fooling ourselves—we have as much as time as there is, eight hours in a normal work day. And everybody has the same amount. "Of course," we can reason. "They can stay late to finish everything. But I have my children to take care of." The problem with that assumption is that other people may not have children, but they have other things to do with their time. They have made a choice, as you have. The issue here is one of making choices, not bemoaning lack of time.

The next time you feel overwhelmed by everything that you have to do, focus on the choices you have made to bring you to this state. What were the events that led up to this? What decision did you make? Could different decisions have changed anything? "Oh, but my hands were tied," and "certain things just couldn't be put off any longer," and "if I didn't do them I would not be able to forgive myself," you may say. But those answers are just taking the focus off yourself. Even if your hands really were tied (and taking the metaphor literally shows us to what lengths we will go to avoid responsibility!), blaming time is meaningless. The hours of your day are not going to suddenly increase—and the sooner you realize this the better off you will be.

To see what a difference this can make, imagine life where

you don't make time the enemy. Think of yourself at work doing a particular task. Later, you are interrupted by a small crisis. You are not pleased, but you take care of the matter and go back to what you were doing earlier. Looking at your watch, you realize it's time to leave for an appointment you have previously made. This means you can't finish what you are doing, and you have to make a quick calculation on whether to take the work home. You and your wife have dinner plans, but you'd like to finish the work tonight. You make a decision: this dinner is important to your wife and you realize you can finish the work tomorrow if you make that extra effort to keep the office door really closed and stay late the following day if necessary. You don't take the work home, you enjoy the dinner with your wife, and decide to take an earlier train the next morning to get an early start on your project.

It's not a perfect solution, because putting anything off is fraught with the possibility that more interruptions may occur. But that is not the point. Even though you are pressured, you keep focused on what you want to do. You have effectively juggled your schedule to the best of your abilities. The shift in perception is subtle but makes a real difference. The minute you start thinking that you have to do everything, that you have no choice, that you wish there were more hours in the day, you create tension for yourself. Worrying in this way takes up energy, which in itself takes up time. Working within your schedule relieves you of added tension and leaves you freer to deal with what really needs to be done. If you think of time as the enemy, it will be; if you learn to think of it as something to work with instead of against, it will suddenly seem less threatening.

2. How Do You Work With Time?

Chances are that you have developed certain patterns and habits with regard to time. What are they? How do you find yourself behaving when it comes to time? Where do you think you can improve? Take a look at some common scenarios:

- You feel you never have enough time for all the tasks you have to do.
- Everything takes longer than you anticipate
- Time always seems to run away from you (you are always playing catch-up)
- You're always late
- You don't make good use of the time you have

How many of these problems areas apply to you? How do they seem to affect your life? And most important, what can you do about solving the problems and turning them into good time management techniques?

The recurrent feeling of a lack of time is often a function of the expectations you have placed on yourself. Generally, the thought process goes like this: I have to do *a, b,* and *c.* And I have *x* amount of time in which to do these things. I know that there's not enough time to do them all, which makes me frustrated and angry. But since I have to get them done, I'll do so as quickly as I can, trying not to think about how upset I am. Maybe I'll feel better tomorrow.

Chances are, however, you won't feel better tomorrow. If you reason that way today, there's an even greater chance you'll reason the same way tomorrow, as you try to finish some leftover tasks as well as straining to fit in new ones. The first question to ask yourself is whether you indeed have to do *a, b,* and *c.* If you feel that you're cramming too much in, why are you trying to do more? Isn't it more fruitful to examine the tasks that you have set for yourself to see if you have been realistic? Perhaps one of them doesn't need to be done, or someone else can do it, or it can be done at a later date. Instead of blaming time, look at your agenda and determine why you have put so much on your plate.

If you're one of those people for whom everything seems to take longer than expected, it means you are not properly estimating the time things take to get done. Often this has to do with not wanting to accept how long a task will take. Although some people are better attuned to the flow of time than others, through experience you know about how much time certain things take to do. You get a feel for them. Follow that gut instinct. For example, you've written budgetary reports over the years and it's always taken you about three weeks, though your predecessor used to do them in two. Preparing to write one again this year, you tell yourself you will finally do it in two weeks as it "should" be done. However, you would be wise to allot three weeks again. Fooling yourself and believing that you will do it "better" is a trap. If something concrete had changed about the report, for example, if someone else had been assigned to write half of it this year, then you would have reason to believe your own work could go faster. But pretending it will be done more quickly because you feel badly about how long it actually does take is not a realistic appraisal of time. Don't blame time instead of accepting responsibility for your own feelings.

Taking on too many tasks or not wanting to admit, realistically, how long things take to do often causes us to feel that time is always running away from us. If you find yourself thinking this way, perhaps you should more accurately ask whether it's not time but you yourself who are running away. And from what? Why do you have to do more of something or do it faster? What are the reasons for feeling badly about what you do accomplish in whatever time it takes you? Examine these reasons. You may be surprised and find that what you think are problems with time are really problems with your own feelings of self worth.

Always being late is usually a function of trying to hold on to that time you always feel is running away. If you're regularly late to meetings, with deadlines, to the job itself, you can't keep blaming traffic, unrealistic schedules, or the fact that you have too much to do. Being late is a statement to everyone else that somehow you don't have enough time in your life. But why not? Have you given yourself too much to do, or are you accepting the pressure of your work without finding a solution? These things may be true during certain periods of your life and in certain cases, but if you find yourself being late with everything, it is time to dig deeper and examine the underlying issues that may be involved.

3. What Is Your Energy Profile?

Recognizing your peak energy periods and making the best use of them translates into good use of time. By now, it is common knowledge that some of us work better in the morning, others in the afternoon, still others at night. Unfortunately, the business world is set up on the nine-to-five schedule and most of us have learned to adapt to it, whether it suits our internal body clock or not. This standardization is certainly reasonable, given the needs of the fast-paced modern world and our desire to get things done efficiently. However, it also means that many of us are not working at peak capacity.

Someday, perhaps, the business world will be more flexible in terms of time—both in hours of the day and days of the week scheduled for business. There are already moves in that direction by various industries as firms experiment with shorter work weeks and longer days, job sharing possibilities, and other alternatives to the traditional work week. Until these new trends take hold, however, the tried-and-true structures will stay in place. If you do not feel you operate well on a nine-to-five schedule, one possibility, of course, is to get out of that mode altogether and find a job with nontraditional hours. However, most jobs that offer flexible hours also tend to be out of the mainstream of the business world, and you are therefore limiting yourself if you are trying to climb the corporate ladder.

Even within this somewhat confining framework, however, there are certain things you can do to make better use of the peaks and valleys in your energy levels. In the first place, learn to recognize your energy cycle. Over the course of a few days, pay attention to the times you feel up and motivated. Contrast them to the times you feel tired. Include weekends. Do any patterns emerge? Take a look and see when you took on the activities that demanded a lot of effort. Focus on your own enjoyment of things. When do you like doing strenuous activities, whether mental or physical? And when do you fantasize about napping or lying on a hammock on some Caribbean island? All these things should give you clues as to when your energy levels are up or down.

Once you've recognized your peak operating hours, you can better integrate them into your working day. If you're a morning person, try and do what takes up most of your energy during those hours. You might not always be able to perform activities of your own choosing—meetings, for example, are often regularly scheduled in the mornings under the assumption that participants will be most alert during that time. Even so, if the meetings occur once or twice a week, you still have three mornings in which to do heavier work, such as writing reports, doing budgetary calculations, or whatever other task seems difficult. The important thing is to plan ahead and set aside the time for these activities. If you wait till you feel up or motivated, it is too easy to fall victim to the "when/whenever" syndrome and end up doing them at the last minute.

4. How Important Is Your Time vs. the Time of Others

How you regard your time as opposed to the time of others gives insight as to how you value yourself. If you find that you always respond to the requests of others before you take care of what you have to do, you would do well to remember that your time is as valuable as everybody else's. Do you treat it as such?

One way to determine this is to gauge how you respond to interruptions. Say you are working on something that's fairly routine though a bit involved—that is, something that takes more energy than simply filing a memo but is also not as stressful as preparing for a major presentation you may give once or twice a year. Perhaps it's a report you put out once a week or a letter you are typing to a client. A coworker calls you and asks for a bit of information that requires some searching through your files. What do you do?

- write the request down and put the paper aside to get to later
- stop what you're doing and search until you find the answer
- start searching, realize that it will take a bit longer than you anticipated, and put the request aside to finish what you're doing first
- ask some questions while still on the phone to determine why the information is needed and who needs it, then decide what you will do
- politely agree to the request without writing it down then put it out of your mind until you can "deal" with it

The responses indicate various levels of concern about your time as opposed to that of others. If you immediately get up and start searching without a thought as to why you are doing it, you obviously consider your coworker's time more valuable than your own. If you start the search then stop, it means your first impulse is still to worry about others before yourself, though after a few minutes' searching you do recognize that your work matters also. The last response of putting the request out of your mind is at the other extreme. You don't think the caller merits even the few seconds of your time that it would take to write down the request. And never mind about doing the work—it's been banished to when/ whenever territory. Writing down the request to do it later is appropriate if the caller hasn't stated an immediate need for the information. Asking a few questions of your own, however, shows not only the healthiest respect for your time and that of your coworker but also good organization on your part. You won't have to call back and ask those questions later.

Observe your reactions to situations like the one above. Make a note of them over a period of time. You may be surprised and find that you are always reacting in one way, at one extreme or the other. If you take a few seconds to judge each case individually, at the outset, perhaps asking questions or requesting that the caller give you some additional information, it means that you value both your time and theirs equally.

5. How Strict Are You About Time?

Are you always on time? How angry do you get when coworkers deliver work late? What is your response to people who show up late for appointments, to meetings, for a lunch date? To you, is being five minutes late as bad as being a half hour late?

Good time management demands flexibility. Although it may seem otherwise, making the best use of time does not mean becoming superefficient—it means having the flexibility to work well with the people around you and the different circumstances in which you find yourself. Life is not neat and easy, and neither is working with time. Some things take longer than anticipated, some people are very bad users of time, and your task is to consider the unexpected time constraints and delays while still getting done what needs to be done.

How do you tell if you're too strict with time? If you're constantly placing demands upon yourself or others that you can't meet, if you're always frustrated with your own inadequacies, or feel angry at those of others, examine why this pattern repeats itself. Creating unreasonable deadlines may be a way to spur yourself and others on to better work, but if it includes frustration and failure, then the method is backfiring. Perhaps you are trying to prove something or are playing a power game with time. What is it? Your authority? Your competence? Turning time into a symbol of power is a dangerous trap—you tend to lose sight of the work itself. If you have made time more important than the work, then you've forgotten why you're on the job in the first place.

Being too nonchalant about time creates problems because you leave everything to chance, letting work get done haphazardly. Not only is this inefficient, it indicates that you don't value your efforts or those of anybody else. If you're constantly late or afraid to set deadlines for others, it may mean you are afraid to take responsibility for your job and the authority you have to get things done. It may mask resentment toward the job you are currently doing. Or it may reflect apathy or laziness. Watch out for those situations when time has become an issue. Good time management means you make a reasonable inventory of whatever work is before you, and then get it done with a minimum of fuss. Time should be used to facilitate work, not impede its progress.

6. How Does Your Company Treat Time?

The next time things get hectic, force yourself to take a minute and ask yourself what has led to the time crunch you find yourself in. But instead of focusing on your behavior, focus on everyone else's. Take your entire company into account and notice how everybody else treats time. This is not so much to let you off the hook as to help you work with your environment and make decisions regarding what can and cannot be changed.

How important are schedules in your company? Does your boss respect your schedules? How do those in charge react when you inform them that something will be late? Is lateness tolerated in general? To what degree? If you start paying attention to those around you, you may realize that even though you are trying your hardest to remain on schedule with whatever you do, the way your company functions makes it impossible. You are not given information when you need it. There may be talk of being on time, but nothing is done when things are late. Instead of cooperation, there is friction among various departments. Acknowledging this does let you off the hook in the sense of putting your own efforts into perspective. Maybe your environment is so bad that, no matter how well you work with time, your efforts will have little effect.

Also ask yourself where your company is on the organizational scale. Are things chaotic or too bureaucratic? How long do routine tasks take to get done? When your company is too much on the chaotic side, things get done quickly, but there always seems to be a sense of panic in the air. Whatever benefits are gained by the fast pace are quickly offset by the disorganization that has been created and the never-ending feelings of frustration and jumping from one project to another. Bureaucracy creates logjams and frustrations of another sort as people waste time inquiring about late invoices, lost memos and unfinished projects. Again, you can do your part in keeping your time as organized as possible, but there may be pressures on you coming from either extreme. Make an effort to learn what can be changed and what has to be accepted. And take one thing at a time, not trying to change the whole company at once. It's not your responsibility to make radical changes, but to be effective in your job.

Finally, a good indication of how your company works with time is how everyone tolerates interruptions. Who interrupts whom? How often? Does everyone have an open door? How much time do you waste in front of your boss's open door while he or she is with someone else? How much time do people waste standing in front of your door? If everyone is used to interrupting everyone else, chances are that creating time for yourself will not be easy. You will either have to learn to live with the situation or seriously consider getting another job.

3

Wasting Time: Looking Beneath the Surface

We all waste time and we all complain about it, yet doing something about it always seems to be a different matter entirely. Learning to see when our time is wasted and understanding some of our reasons for doing so will better enable us to make the changes that we want to make in our time management skills.

Consider the different ways you waste time at work. Before you put your list together, however, keep one thing in mind. Take a look at how you define wasted time. You may find that you are unnecessarily blaming yourself for a bad use of time when in fact what you are referring to are routine or boring tasks that have to get done as part of your job. No one else can do them, they can't be done any differently—they are integral to your work. That is not a bad use of time. That is just an acceptance of the fact that every job will have certain boring or repetitious tasks which are unavoidable. Examples of such tasks are:

- processing certain forms such as invoices, time sheets, or any forms that move work along from one department to another
- putting out a report on a periodic basis
- answering phone inquiries that revolve around one specific topic
- going to regularly scheduled meetings at which the same things are discussed

Often, of course, with new technology, some of these tasks can be changed or at least partially eliminated with the help of computers and telephone voice mail. But if you feel these possibilities have been adequately investigated and nothing can be changed for the time being, you should stop blaming yourself for a bad use of time. This is not wasted time. This is part of your job. Short of changing your job entirely, there is nothing you can do about such tasks.

There are routine things you do, however, that are clearly a waste of time because by doing them you are not accomplishing anything directly related to your job. As boring as it is, filling in an invoice moves the work along, however inefficiently. But such activities as the ones in the list below are at best an interruption and sometimes even keep the work from getting done at all. They are your little personal time wasters:

- interrupting whatever you're doing by constantly remembering certain other tasks that have to be done immediately
- making small talk with someone who comes by your office or desk

- getting coffee (or food, or cigarettes) and leaving most of it unfinished so that in a few minutes you have to get a new cup
- waiting for inspiration to start instead of getting down to work
- feeling so overwhelmed with everything you have to do that you do nothing
- complaining about how much work you have instead of doing what you can
- Waiting outside the boss' office if he/she is busy instead of completing your own work

As opposed to the things in the previous list, these activities are not necessary—certainly not on a constant or routine basis. Identify ones that you are prone to. Once you start thinking about them, you can find them everywhere. Remember, the main point is not that you do them occasionally but that they have become part of your job—even though they serve no purpose in it.

Hidden Agendas

Having identified your personal time wasters, you want to ask yourself why you do them. Often there is an underlying need or an unstated reason which is the motivating force behind minutes wasted in this way. Ask yourself what the reasons— the hidden agendas—may be. Think about the benefits you may derive from these modes of behavior, why you are so willing to fool yourself into thinking that they serve a useful purpose.

- Avoidance. As we've discussed, we usually prefer to do things that take up less energy. See if there is a pattern to your time wasters regarding this issue. Do you often waste time before certain tasks that seem overwhelming? Are the tasks really difficult or is it just your perception of them? Do you avoid work having to do with certain people or departments? Is it because you perceive the people as difficult or your work as not adequate enough? Maybe you feel you are psyching yourself up for a tough task. If you are, you'll have to make a decision: Can you justify the time taken with this process or, as is more usually the case, can you work on lessening the time wasters once you realize that you are actually wasting energy by not starting the work sooner.

- Resentment. Are you angry about what you have to do? Do you feel you are doing someone else's job? Or is it that you feel you are too experienced or too overloaded to engage in certain projects? Or maybe you feel you are not experienced enough and are being unfairly taken advantage of? First of all, decide whether you are upset about certain aspects of what you do or your job as a whole. And talk to your boss, who may be able to help you make some changes. If you're still not satisfied, investigate other jobs within the company. If nothing seems to be available, you should start making serious plans to look for other work. The longer you stay at a job that you resent, the more time you'll waste and the angrier you'll get at both yourself and those with whom you work.

- Pleasure. Sometimes you'll find you do certain things for their own sake—you like to do them. Examine this satisfaction, maybe it indicates certain talents or aspirations that you are not acknowledging. For example, if you are constantly going around talking to everyone in the company when you have something to discuss instead of calling them by phone, you probably enjoy the interaction. Perhaps you are in the wrong job, which involves too much paperwork and doesn't give you enough people contact so that you search it out on your own. In such a situation, you may justify your time wasting on the grounds that you're making the best out of an imperfect situation. Or, this realization may point you to a new job or career altogether.

- Self sabotage. Not getting down to business may mask conflicts you have about getting ahead. Perhaps you're not as ambitious as you would like to believe because you're either afraid of the added responsibilities a promotion may bring or you just don't want the hassle. Instead of admitting this to yourself openly, you sabotage yourself in little ways to keep from getting ahead. The satisfaction in this case is being able to stay right where you are.

- Exhaustion. You may be just plain tired. If you find yourself engaging in these activities after a big project, you may be telling yourself you are not ready to take on something else that is strenuous. A good solution may be to do some of those boring, routine tasks that need to get done anyway. The time wasting activities can also be a way of using up excess energy—if you're still on a high from an involving but particularly satisfying project, wasting time in this manner may be a way of calming yourself so that you can clear your mind and get on to other things.

Procrastination

More of us feel we waste time procrastinating than on anything else. Procrastinating is wasting time by putting off a particular activity that we feel should be done now. However, we find ways to push it off until later. Yet eventually it does get done, after much frustration, anxiety, and guilt. Once we look back, we see that these feelings have wasted our time. We have let them fill up—and thus waste—our precious hours, as we focus our attention on the feelings instead of getting to the task at hand.

The underlying emotion of procrastination is often fear. We are afraid to start something because we are not sure of our abilities to do it properly. Perhaps we are in the habit of asking too much of ourselves. Perhaps we don't think we've been trained adequately enough. Sometimes our insecurities stem from the fact that we focus on the entire project—its importance, its complexity, its difficulty—and are intimidated, feeling overwhelmed.

The hidden agendas mentioned above can also come into play. We put off a task because we resent it, thinking it rightly shouldn't be assigned to us. Or we just want to avoid it because it may require hard work and bring up unpleasant feelings or cause confrontations with other staff members. Before we can "get over" these kinds of blocks, we have to acknowledge them as part of human nature and not blame ourselves for having them. It's a rare person who enjoys firing employees or confronting someone because of bad attitude; we would think there's something not quite right about a person who actually relished such things.

Procrastination is also a symptom of needing to feel in control. Whether we procrastinate out of fear or resentment, by not doing something we are making a statement. And that statement is, "I will do this task when I *decide* to do it. Not before." Never mind that this decision causes stress; we are willing to put up with all the negative feelings for some sense of control. It gives us security. As always, blaming ourselves and demanding that we get over it will not work. Instead, we should look at why we feel we need to make such a decision in the first place.

A particular twist to procrastination is having difficulty starting. Often, once we've finally begun the work and have lost ourselves in it, it goes fairly smoothly, and we wonder what the fuss was all about. If starting is your problem, you are probably letting the task overwhelm you, as you think about its importance instead of doing it. You've probably attached a lot of significance to this task—it means so much to you to do it right—and the significance overwhelms the work itself. You put off the work, the anxiety increases, which in turn increases the significance even further, and you find yourself in a vicious cycle.

Sometimes we are unnecessarily hard on ourselves and confuse procrastination with time used for thinking. The need to generate ideas when we are creating something or to come up with solutions for particularly complex problems is a process that needs "percolating" time. Sometimes this means just sitting quietly and staring out the window, letting the ideas come and go. Consider it as browsing around in your subconscious. Notice that this quiet time does not mean reading the newspaper or engaging in some other pleasant, unrelated activity. The mind is focused on the task at hand, though you are being more open and relaxed, allowing the ideas to come to you without putting any particular schedule on them.

Once you have recognized the way in which you procrastinate, you can start to make some changes. As you strive not to put off things, however, remember that this habit is usually strongly ingrained—procrastination lets you avoid some deep, unpleasant feelings. So expect the changes to come slowly—which is not to discourage you, but to give you the wherewithal to keep trying. To help yourself, consider the following pointers:

- Do it bit by bit. Instead of focusing on the entire project, break it down into smaller entities. If you are writing something, try writing down your thoughts randomly at first. If you are doing calculations, don't worry at this point how they will all come together. Worry about each individual formula first.

- Stop focusing on the project's importance. The more you think your job is riding on a particular project, the more it will be. It's not a good way of putting pressure on yourself. And don't blow the job out of proportion as far as your company is concerned. Chances are the company will survive even if you don't do well; focus on the job and due credit will take care of itself.

- Promise yourself a reward if you finish something on time. It's a gimmick, but one that works. Instead of focusing on the difficulties of the task, you've created something pleasant on which to put your expectations: the upcoming vacation, wearing the new dress, zooming down the slope on those new skis.

- Allow yourself to make mistakes. Keep reminding yourself that mistakes are part of the learning process— you almost have to make mistakes to learn. If your boss or coworkers don't tolerate them, there is something wrong with them, not you.

- Never be afraid of asking questions. Allowing yourself to make mistakes includes allowing yourself to admit that you don't know something. It's a sign of strength rather than weakness if you are able to ask for help. All of us have wasted time doing something the wrong way or to the wrong specifications simply by not asking questions. To help yourself speak up the next time a similar situation occurs, remind yourself of the time you wasted previously. If those around you don't tolerate questions, start looking for another job.

Perfectionism

Perfectionism is particularly dangerous because it can feel so good. There we are, striving to do our best, keeping at it, not caring how much time it takes because doing it right is our first priority. Unfortunately, we confuse doing it right with doing it perfectly. No mistakes allowed. Everything has to fit just so—even as we're doing it. And the more we try to make it just so, the more the perfection eludes us. It becomes a vicious cycle of wasted time.

Just like procrastination, perfectionism is used to justify insecurities. For whatever reason, we don't feel good enough, so to make up for it, whatever we do must be beyond reproach. Getting praise for a job perfectly done momentarily assuages our feelings of imperfection—but not for long. The smallest criticism can set us off on the vicious cycle again as we feel we have to make up for whatever new thing we did wrong.

Unfortunately, the competitive climate in so many industries today fosters perfectionism all too easily. Equating their own self-worth with their jobs, many men and women throw themselves wholeheartedly into their careers, imagining that if they don't do it perfectly someone else will come along who will. The line between healthy competition and self-abuse is lost.

How can you tell if you have crossed that line? It is not easy, because it requires seeing through something that seems so right at first. After all, isn't it better to strive to do one's best than to do one's worst? But that is not the point. Someone who is a perfectionist takes that striving for the best to such a degree that very little, if anything, he or she does is acceptable. So they don't let themselves off the hook until forced to by circumstances that include burnout, physical maladies, and more often than not, acute emotional illnesses.

Take a look at the symptoms of perfectionism listed

below. If they define how you function at work, start taking a serious inventory of yourself to see how you can stop yourself from going down that dangerous track.

- Obsessiveness. Perfectionism has a feeling of sameness to it—you do the same thing over and over until you get it right. The telling point is that it doesn't matter whether the task is big or small. There's no variation— you do everything the same way.
- Inability to stop work. You can't give your boss a letter you've typed, you can't stop tinkering with the organizational chart until every *i* is dotted and every *t* is crossed. If there's even a single mistake, you have to do it all over again.
- Work backlog. You constantly have work piling up on your desk or are taking it home because you haven't completed previously assigned tasks. However, when your boss attempts to question you about them in seeing if the load can be lightened, you pretend there is nothing wrong.
- Overplanning. If you are preparing to work on a big project, you gather data, make outlines, read books and theses—and never feel you've done enough to start the actual work. So you hide behind the planning and outlining and researching as an excuse not to start the work itself.
- Working under pressure. You convince yourself you always work best under the gun. Working under pressure may be better than not getting the job done at all, but needing the extra stimulation on a constant basis is not a good sign. The pressure doesn't help the work; it creates a distraction.
- Inability to relax. You think enjoying yourself is a waste of time. Or even worse, you fantasize about

doing something fun, but you somehow can't—the
excuses not to do it always seem greater than the
reasons for it.

- Not taking advice. When you can't distinguish between well-meaning advice and meddling, when you
always know better than anybody, when you take any
criticism as a personal insult, then your perfectionism
is in control of you. As hard as it is, do whatever you
can to examine why you feel the way you do. In the
long run it will save not only your time but your health
and emotional well-being as well.

Doing the Immediate vs. the Important

Don't confuse the immediate with the important. The immediate tasks consist of all the little emergencies and problems
that come up during the course of a normal day. In one sense,
that's what we are getting paid for—to be at our desks or in
our offices and to answer questions, carry out requests, take
care of paperwork, and in general help see to it that our part
of the organization's work is running smoothly. However,
that's not all we're getting paid for. Whatever job we're in, we
all have tasks that do not have to be done immediately but
which we consider more important over the long run. Whether
you're the secretary who wants to reorganize the files, or the
manager who wants to write the long-overdue memo justify-
ing salary increases for your department, you know you want
to do these things—you just can't seem to find the time to do
them.

Like so much else having to do with time management,
this problem stems from human nature. Our desire for instant
gratification is always present to some degree, and when it is
reinforced by life around us, we often give in to it. Filling up

our day with little things—what many time experts call the busyness syndrome—gives us a feeling of satisfaction in the short run, though in the long run we feel that we have cheated ourselves. It is easy for us to do this for many reasons:

- Confusing the two is easy. Something immediate is important—very important—at that moment. The problem is that your day may be composed of many such moments. You have to look at the bigger picture and make choices. Asking yourself why you are doing something helps distinguish between the important and the merely immediate. Try it the next time you are rushing around, feeling overwhelmed. You may be surprised and find that you are carrying out a request blindly to please the powers that be instead of confronting the truth that the request is unnecessary, inefficient, or can be done differently.

- Important tasks tend to be vague, more encompassing, while the immediate ones are specific and clear. The more important something is, the less defined and further off in the future it tends to be. If you find yourself putting off an important task, try to define it and clarify the steps involved in accomplishing it. If necessary, start by concentrating on one aspect of the task.

- The deadlines are usually vague or there aren't any deadlines at all. It's another aspect of human nature— if we don't have deadlines, we tend not to do something until the deadline appears. If at all possible, set up some kind of schedule for yourself, taking things one step at a time.

- You have to do it yourself. Another reason why the important things go undone is that we have no one breathing down our necks, whip in hand, telling us we will be fired if we don't get cracking. Self-motivation is always difficult.

- It's easier to be passive. Doing something important means taking an active role in our lives. As we've discussed, the passive path is always more tempting. While you're struggling with motivation, give yourself some pats on the back—you're not doing something easy.

Being Effective vs. Efficient

Another question to ask yourself as you are completing tasks or fulfilling requests is: Am I being effective or efficient? Asking this question goes hand in hand with determining what is important as opposed to what needs to be done immediately. The question is a way of focusing on yourself, however, rather than on the task at hand, and so is another method of looking at your behavior as the deciding factor in good—or wasteful—use of time.

Think of the difference between the two words. Effective implies that you get things done—things that you want to do. Efficient implies that you do tasks well, with little waste, whatever these tasks may be. Being effective entails making decisions, taking charge, while being efficient entails simply completing an activity, without much thought to the overall picture.

By being effective, you do what's important to you. Because such a task may be less well-defined than a task which you can quickly—efficiently—get done, it is easy to put off or not do at all. Efficiency produces a great feeling. You've done twenty things today and you're very proud of yourself. Being efficient is a good quality to have, but not at the expense of effectiveness. If you are in a management position, for example, and always insist on making your own reservations for traveling to international conventions—because you can do it better than your secretary—you are being efficient but not very effective. There are probably many other ways in which you can be using your time that would be more beneficial to your company.

The two qualities don't have to be mutually exclusive. If you are being effective—working on something that is important—and you are doing it efficiently, that is the best of both possible worlds. It is when you are blinded by efficiency and the instant gratification which it supplies that you are not making good use of your time. Is it important? Are you being effective? Or does it fall into the category of immediate, and are you being merely efficient? Use those questions effectively and efficiently whenever you need to make a judgment call about what you are doing. They should help steer you in the right direction.

PART TWO

MAKING THE BEST USE OF TIME

4

Planning Time: Taking Control of Your Day

Planning is taking the knowledge that we have to manage ourselves instead of time and consciously doing something with that realization. Planning is the way we "find" time, acknowledging that time will never spontaneously become available to us if we don't take matters into our own hands. Planning our work day, just like planning for life in general, consists of taking control of the events of the day. It means that we don't allow others to run our day for us. It means that we make ourselves the prime decision-makers of what can or should be done. And it means that we respect ourselves enough to do it.

Only you can take control of your day, because you are best acquainted with your needs and your job. What may work for one person may not work for you. This ability to count on yourself is a prime consideration in being able to plan adequately.

This does not mean, of course, that you don't work with others. Listening to someone else's opinion, weighing what you know against what they tell you, and taking your own needs into account are all factors in the decision-making process.

In planning, watch out for the following traps:

- Don't overplan. Remind yourself that planning something is not actually doing it. The plan facilitates the work but does not substitute for it. Think of an outline, which helps shape a book or report; at some point, however, the actual writing has to begin.
- Don't be afraid of yourself. Overplanning can be a sign of perfectionism. If you keep doing research or tinkering with an outline, you may become afraid to begin. The importance of having confidence in your abilities can't be emphasized enough. At some point you have to let go of the planning and start the work.
- Don't spend all of your time on that last, difficult-to-get piece of information. If you've gathered the majority of research material for that report but feel you still lack a few things, don't spend hours tracking them down. In doing the work, you may find that you don't actually need all the missing links. Or you may decide you need others. The search will be much more efficient further down the road.

Setting Goals and Having Priorities

The first step in planning is knowing what you are planning for. You want to have goals, both long-range and short term, and you want to be able to prioritize them. The goals are your decisions on where you will direct your energies, and your priorities are your time maps, helping you decide when to do what.

In deciding on goals, you should first think about what you want to accomplish in the long run. A long-range goal is one overall achievement that is important to you. If you are a secretary, you may want to fill your boss's shoes someday. If you are a manager, you may want to fill the president's. If you are the president, you think that a position as CEO of the conglomerate which owns your company is not such an impossible wish. Having a long-range goal is having a vision for yourself and your job. You use it as a guide for everything else that you do.

Your short-run goals all point to this overall goal and help you in its realization. Think of these goals as specific ways that you can reach your overall goal. If you are the manager hoping to become president of the company, for example, you may decide that a promotion to vice president in the next two years is your next reasonable step toward that end. Becoming vice president will entail other, shorter-term goals: increasing the productivity of your department, making more money for the company, solving any existing organizational problems. You devise even more specific goals toward those ends. And this is how it works—taking each goal and breaking it down into ever smaller ones, always keeping focused on the ultimate outcome.

As you pick out your goals, you also need to decide how important each one is and when it should be done. Prioritizing is necessary because you have only limited resources, whether it's time or energy or anything else. You will decide what should be done first, taking into consideration the goals you have come up with, what you think it will take to realize them, and how they fit into the overall structure of your job and your company.

Prioritizing can take some juggling as life is never clean-cut. For example, as a supervisor of a department, you may feel that your worst problem is an overlap in duties among your staff. Correcting that problem is your first priority. However, you are also waiting to hire another employee, but your request has been held up. Before you can best determine who should do what, you need to know whether you will have an extra person working for you.

You can either do nothing until that decision is made, or do a partial evaluation of the work flow, or try to work on the other problems. Making this decision will involve a judgment call. You have to think of the various factors involved—how long will the decision on the new employee take? how bad are the other problems? are there other emergencies to deal with?—and make your decision based on how each problem affects the other ones. The important thing to remember is that, ideally, correcting the first problem should help you in working on the second, which should help you on your next one, and so on. The more such a progression can be followed, the better you are at using your time.

Prioritizing also includes adaptability. Your overall goal won't change too often, if at all, but your shorter-term goals will. Conditions in your office may change. You may get promoted. There may be a financial squeeze. Through all of this you have to keep checking up on yourself to make sure that your goals reflect a true picture of reality. If you find out that there will be a financial squeeze in the following year, you have to decide whether you have to fight harder for that extra person you need, or whether you should save your energies for something else and live with a smaller staff.

Your Time Diary

In order to help yourself better plan your time, you first want to know exactly how you spend it. That's where keeping a diary comes in. You may think you know where the time goes, but there is a world of difference between writing it down and keeping it your head. First of all, no matter how good your memory is, you will be bound to forget certain things. We pick and choose what we want to remember, usually preferring the more pleasant memories. Seeing something in black-and-white confirms what may be too easy to brush aside. And secondly, writing something down forces you to think about what you are doing. Even that small effort may be enough to get you to make some changes.

Keep the time diary over a period of a few days, or a whole week if possible. And be careful of waiting for a "normal" week, which can turn into a time waster in itself. Many things can be turned into excuses for never finding that week which seems normal. Apart from several special occasions during the year, such as conferences, inventory time, and end-of-year budgetary close-outs, most of your weeks will suffice quite nicely. The important thing is to keep the diary, not wait for the perfectly average week.

In keeping the diary, remember the following:

- jot down the time and the activity
- start with the first thing you do in the morning and finish with your last activity before leaving
- write down the events as they're happening
- be honest, not calling socializing "thinking" or "creative respite"
- be brief
- be objective
- don't include value judgments, such as "another half hour forced to listen to that chatterbox"

After a few days' time, you are ready to make an inventory of what you've written down. You may be shocked at first, as many people are who realize they've spent much more time than they imagined on a particularly inconsequential activity, such as playing telephone tag. This may be a time waster, or it may not, depending on how it is used. The point is, we often pick certain activities to give ourselves the illusion of working, though what we are really doing is soothing our egos, resting, avoiding particular projects and tasks, deflecting worry about something that may be bothering us, pretending we're busy when we're really not. An activity such as this has become so ingrained, we don't even notice we are doing it. The time diary forces us to see it more clearly.

In analyzing your time diary, pay attention to interruptions. How many did you cause as opposed to the number that were forced on you? And notice how much time you spent on work that you initiated as opposed to requests from your coworkers or boss. It will give you a good indication of how in control of your day you really are. And what about patterns? Your time diary can be a good indicator of your energy cycle. Pay particular attention to how much time is usually takes you to get started on projects. That's often another shocker, as people find they are only performing certain activities as a prelude to starting the "real" work.

Your time diary is invaluable in sorting out reality from fantasy. Looking at an objective list of how you spent your day does away with illusions and excuses. There are your hours, in black-and-white. Don't look at it as judging yourself, but as a useful tool to sort out what you think you are doing from how you are really spending your time at a given moment.

Keeping a "To Do" List

A "To Do" list is the rudder that keeps you on course. Just as keeping a time diary gives you a clearer picture of where the time goes, writing down what you want to do with your time gives more purpose to your day. A "To Do" list is an organizing tool. It keeps you focused on the important things. It's also a motivator, reminding you right there in black and white of what needs to be done.

A "To Do" list should be done every day. Do it every morning, looking at it as a few minutes of "pre-work" planning, thinking, and easing into your office routine. Or do it at 5 P.M. for the following day. Although leaving anything for last is dangerous because your energies are low and it is much easier to put things off, if you can stick to it, it becomes a good way of quickly reviewing your day as well as planning in advance.

Just like a time diary, a "To Do" list should not be complicated. It is a list, which means that it is brief and succinct. It consists of notes to yourself, incomplete sentences and short phrases rather than detailed instructions. It should fit on one sheet of a legal-sized pad. And as you are doing it, you should always keep priorities in mind, listing the most important things first, then crossing them out as you finish the tasks and adding new ones.

Some people prefer a little more organization, dividing the list into sections based on various aspects of their job, or the different departments they work with or coworkers with whom they work. The time that something should be done can also be a factor. The thing to remember, however, is that the list is a planning tool, so that you don't want to get bogged down in details or intricacies. The main reason for dividing it into sections is that this gives you an immediate visual clue regarding the nature of the task you have jotted down.

Simplify the list if keeping it starts taking more time that it saves.

And always remember the Rule of Ones: Keep one list and keep it in one place so that you always know where it is. If you have notes on scraps of paper, transfer them to the list when you are going over it. This does not mean you have to necessarily recopy every bit of information you may have taken from a phone message or jotted down during a meeting with someone. Write down the basics and file away the scrap so you know where to find it if necessary. It is the time you save searching for information during pressure-filled moments that can make so much difference during the course of a hectic day.

The Importance of Systems

Systems save time—a lot of time. They allow you to do things automatically so that you don't have to spend time figuring out how to carry out certain routine tasks. Once you have a system in place you can perform a particular job almost reflexively, not worrying about the many details associated with it. As your time diary will show, seemingly inconsequential details matter greatly. If not taken care of in a systematic way, they have a way of mushrooming and creating more work and wasted time. You can waste precious minutes wondering who to call for what information, answering such questions by others, trying to decide what comes next in a particular series of tasks, or rushing to get something done only to realize that something else should have been done first.

Having a system facilitates any job, whether done by one person or several. It can be created for something as personal as how a secretary responds to requests by her boss to how people communicate on a big project with dozens of workers in various departments. Communication in a system involving

more than one person is important because the primary aim of
having a system is to clearly delineate the flow of work so that
there is no overlap and confusion. Organization is also a
key—everything has its place. A good system is not rigid,
however, and always allows for flexibility and changes in
conditions.

In creating any system, whether for yourself or for tasks
that involve other people, first take the time to become
acquainted with the current flow of work. If you are creating
a system for your own job, first note what information comes
to you, the form that it takes, and what you are supposed to
do with it. If you are creating a system that involves others,
notice who does what, how long it takes them to do it, and
how successful the end result seems to be. Trying to change a
system without knowing how it works is never wise. You may
find certain things in the old system that work very well and
which you want to incorporate into the new one. Or you may
find that though it's not perfect, the old system works
adequately enough and that there are other ways you can more
profitably spend your time. Nothing can create more head-
aches than changing a system that does not need to be
changed.

Below are some guidelines to follow in creating any kind
of system. In the example that follows, you are the managing
editor of a publishing company. You are creating a system to
keep everybody adequately informed about the scheduling of
various books.

- A system should have a definite beginning and end, a
  desired result. In this case, you are the beginning and
  everyone outside the company who needs to be kept
  abreast of the schedule is the end. Their up-to-date
  knowledge of what is happening is the desired result.
  In this case you decide the best thing to do is for you
  to put out a memo.

- Think it through sequentially. For example, how will the information that a book has been delayed get from you to a talk show that has booked the author for an appearance to coincide with the publication date? The publicity department is the one which works with talk shows, so you should send a memo to it and expect it to inform the talk show. In the same way, the sales department will inform the bookstore, while the editor will inform the author himself. In this scenario, you have decided that the routing of the memo will be from you (point A) to each department in the company (point B), each of whom will then in turn inform their clients (point C).
- It has to happen automatically. In the examples above, your memo should trigger an automatic response in the various departments. Once you have done your part, you shouldn't have to worry about what point B does or what happens at point C. That is someone else's job.
- Make sure that lines of responsibility are very clear. Things may not happen so automatically if the sales department thinks the publicity department should inform the bookstore. And who informs the author, the author's editor, or the author's publicist? It all has to be spelled out clearly.
- A good system also includes checkpoints. If there is a problem with what is happening, the various checkpoints along the way should serve to alert you to the fact. For example, the subsidiary rights department gets your memo delaying the book. They, however, have sold excerpts of the book to a major magazine, which has to come out at a particular date. If the book is late, the deal is off and your company stands to lose a lot of money. The subsidiary rights people call you up in desperation asking if anything can be done.

Alerted by them, you talk to the people producing the book to see if the situation can be salvaged. Again, it all has happened automatically—you have set up the system so that everyone who needs a copy of the memo gets it. They, in turn, are all well aware of their responsibilities.

• Write it down and keep it for reference. If the system you have created is at all complex, involving several people or areas of responsibility, keep it in written form. First of all, putting it in writing will highlight any missing links that may have been overlooked in the initial planning process. Also, the more complex it is, the more apt a system is to have problems. There may be meetings further down the road in attempting to tinker with the system some more. Having it down on paper will provide a ready reference for all who are participating in making the additional changes.

5

Scheduling, Part One: Do the Most Important Thing First!

If you learn only one thing from reading this book, it should be this: Do the most important thing first! It is fundamental to good use of time, and so significant that it deserves a chapter all by itself. It is the primary tenet of intelligent scheduling.

Scheduling is the nuts and bolts of planning. You have elucidated your goals and priorities for the near and far future and have taken a realistic look at how you spend your work day. Now you want to take this information and use it in the best way possible to maximize the hours at your disposal. Doing the most important thing first starts you off on the right track.

Concentrating on what is most important has to do with

that old bugaboo of human nature, instant gratification. We like to feel good, and it is always tempting to do something for which the reward comes quickly. Usually, however, anything that we consider important will use up more of our energies to accomplish and will provide rewards at a later date—if at all. We succumb to the immediate-vs.-important trap. Therefore, it's easy to make our noble-sounding plans—I will reorganize the office, I will straighten out the department, I will expand the company—and keep putting off these things. The same goes for tasks done a smaller scale—the tasks that we consider the most important for a particular day. They are put off just as easily as the grand schemes.

When you are scheduling your day, the time spent on any particular task is only one factor among many that you take into consideration. Your energy level, your interest, where the task falls on the important-vs.-immediate scale, the possibility of interruptions, the degree of privacy you may need, also play a part. Most of these factors are calculated quickly, almost unconsciously, especially on tasks which are more routine.

However, the more important a task is, the less likely you are to give these factors their due. For example, the most important thing you have to do on a particular day is confront your secretary with a performance review that is not going to be good. What you say to yourself is, "compared to the seriousness of what I have to tell her, my energy level or the way I feel or annoying interruptions by coworkers are inconsequential. I won't plan on them because they shouldn't matter anyway. I have to concentrate on the task at hand." So you schedule your discussion for 4 P.M., wanting to spend the rest of the day doing some more work on landing the big account which will put a real feather in your cap, going to the boring business luncheon to increase your contacts, and coming back to take care of some minor chores. However, what happens is that there are some further complications and the big account suddenly seems in jeopardy, the business luncheon takes longer than anticipated, and you come back angry and unable to concentrate on any tasks at all. Still brooding about the big account, you put off your talk with your secretary because you tell yourself the big account has now become your first priority. And you go home feeling frustrated because the day has "run away" from you again.

What has happened is that your feelings, your energy level, the unforeseen emergencies have played a very real part in your plans—despite your intentions. Your scheduling suddenly seems like an illusion because you didn't take all these things into account. And yet you couldn't have. Some of what happened could not be prevented.

While you cannot control everything, doing the most important thing first minimizes the unpredictability of your day. If you had confronted your secretary first, taking care of that task would have taken away some of the sting of not landing the account. You could also now devote your energies fully to getting the account back. Instead, you not only have to worry about the account, you still have your secretary to deal with. The pressure on you has increased tremendously.

The one argument that many people have with doing the most important thing first is that the beginning of the day may not represent their energy peak. They may feel at their most energetic later in the day and usually schedule whatever is most important for the afternoon, using the first part of the day for undemanding tasks. This argument is valid up to a point, and that point is the nine-to-five schedule of the business world. A lot may happen during the first part of the day and a lot may be expected of you, no matter what your energy cycle is. No matter how hard you try to block off the time later in the day, it can be all too easily compromised. Even if the person in the example above felt at his most energetic during the afternoon, all of the other, seemingly inconsequential factors would have made talking to his secretary difficult. If something seems really important, most late-rising types gather their energies the best they can and do what they have to do early on in the day. Then they allow themselves to collapse. Occasionally, if they can be disciplined about it, they give themselves a certain amount of time, say an hour or so, on easy tasks to "wake up" and prepare themselves for the real work. Until the schedule of the working world changes, these tricks will probably remain the best solutions to a thorny problem.

But even with these difficulties, for most people the benefits of doing the most important thing first far outweigh the problems. Whether you consider yourself an early or a late riser, schedule your important task or project for as early as you can. You will be doing yourself a favor in the following ways:

- It is the best way to deal with the unpredictability of your day. You may think you have it all in control but you never do. Those small things can easily trip you up.
- You will spend the time when you are most alert on what really counts. If you are one of those people who juices don't start flowing until later, you may have to do some adjusting, but stick to it as closely as you can.
- There is a greater chance that what you want to do will match what you really end up doing. Your satisfaction with yourself will increase, which will do wonders for your self-esteem.
- You will use less energy. Any important task includes anticipation, however long you may put it off. You think about the best way to do it, worry whether you will be successful, fantasize about good and bad scenarios. It's easy to forget that all this anticipation takes energy. The sooner you are done with it, the sooner you can use the energy for other things.

- You will be able to use "down" time more efficiently. If you do what is difficult when your energies are high, you still may have some left over to do those easier tasks. If you try for the reverse and do the small tasks when your energies are high, chances are you will not do the difficult thing when your energies are flagging. You will put the task off and "waste" the rest of the day.
- You will be seen as being in control and your work will be noticed. While you never want to plan what you do for show, the more you accomplish the big tasks, the more visible your work tends to be. If you can balance these and still keep on top of the little things, you will be perceived as a good time manager.

6

Scheduling, Part Two: Finding the Balance

The art of scheduling requires knowing how to integrate time spent on the most important thing, as defined in the previous chapter, with time spent on more mundane matters. It's a fine balance, one that includes juggling tasks on a daily basis and scheduling your time around projects that may last weeks or months. It's a balance that you want to incorporate into every working day so that the juggling, whether short- or long-term, becomes second nature to you.

Think of scheduling your time each day as balancing your company's needs against your own. There are routine things to be done. Important tasks to be considered. Unforeseen emergencies that come up. There is also you: How much can you do? Want to do? Feel you should do? How much of it is a struggle and how much is enjoyable? If you are avoiding something, is it because you honestly think it can be put off or are you procrastinating? All these things matter. As you schedule your time day by day, preferably with the aid of a "To Do" list, they will make their influence felt.

The lynchpin of your day is the most important thing you have to do. Hopefully it has been scheduled to be done first. However, the most important thing might also be something over which you don't have much control, for example, an important lunch or meeting in the afternoon. You know you have to attend, and it's not going to be your first activity of the day. If such is the case, you have to decide how best to spend the hours preceding it. You may go over some notes and do a last-minute preparation, though if you have scheduled your time well on previous days you already would have done most of the preparatory work. You should not be spending much time on it now. You will be wiser to try and take your mind off it and concentrate on something fairly important though not quite as involved, so that you can relax while still remaining productive.

Other prescheduled activities will also be part of your day. They also have a high priority—anything that is prescheduled earns that status on your list. Leaving yourself enough time between these prescheduled activities is important. Be careful of making a schedule that is too rigid, of setting too much of what you plan to do by the clock. Your schedule will change so often that you will spend more time revising it than doing the work it represents. As a general rule, two or three activities that you think will take an hour or more, including meetings, a lunch date, seeing a client— including your most important task—will fill up your day very quickly.

Tasks which you consider important but which are not scheduled will further complicate matters. How many of them you get to will depend on their nature and what else happens during the day. This is usually when the important-vs.-immediate dilemma makes itself felt. New problems will threaten to throw your schedule out of whack. Remaining flexible enough to act on the unplanned problems and juggling them with what you've already scheduled will test your time management skills. You have to accept this aspect of your working day. Your defense against it is your prioritizing and knowing that you are in charge—it is up to you decide what is most important during each given moment and to act on it. That is how you keep on top of everything. Let your "To Do" list guide you, knowing that it will always be in a state of flux and making that your advantage, not your downfall.

Long-range projects

There may be times when you get involved in special projects that last much longer than anything you normally do—weeks, months, maybe even a year or more. Scheduling your workload during such periods remains essentially the same as scheduling each day—except your "day" in this case is extended over a long stretch of time. You still have to perform a balancing act, blocking out specific times—maybe entire days or weeks depending on the length of the project—to get certain things accomplished having to do with the project. At the same time you have to do your regular job, being careful that the special project doesn't push it aside. If it does, you will have to know when to ask for help or give up some duties.

Generally, the project will take up less of your time in the beginning and will progress accordingly, eating up more and more of your time as it progresses. In the beginning, it will be in the planning stages as you try to work out systems associated with it. In doing the initial planning, be aware that some things will work themselves out as you go along. Also, aspects of the project will change as it gets going. Accept this. Just as in dealing with the particulars of each day, flexibility will be important. The middle period is often the most confusing, as the end is not yet in sight but the work is coming fast and furiously, and your juggling abilities are put to their greatest test. During the last third of the project—as you do near the end and try to get everything done—more and more of your time will be taken up by it. Plan for this also. It will be balanced out by the fact that by this point you will feel in good control of it, having a better idea of what your end product will be.

This increase in intensity will take place no matter whether you are working on something alone or are involved in a project with many people. If you are coordinating work with others, pay particular attention to the section of the book describing systems. The need for a clear, systematic flow of work is vital.

The need to feel on top of the project by everyone involved is also a prime consideration. It is easy to get demoralized by something that takes so long—especially when the outcome is uncertain and no one feels the project is yet on its way. To combat low morale, always keep in mind the step-by-step approach. Tell yourself—and others—that you are not doing the whole thing right now. Concentrate on one aspect at a time and know that that's all you can do. Plan on periodic celebrations or a relaxation of the pressure once certain portions are completed. They will be good morale boosters for the work to follow.

If you are also doing your regular job in addition to working on the long-term project, watching that your regular job is not pushed aside will be important—especially during that last third when work on the long-term project is at its most concentrated. Plan in advance, watching out for routine projects or tasks that may conflict with the long-term one. Asking for help *before* you feel overwhelmed will allow you to make better preparations. Specify the areas of conflict and your proposed solutions. The more specific you are the more openly your request for help will be received by the powers that be.

In scheduling your time and that of others for maximum effectiveness during a long-term project, you will be juggling work, calendar, and day-to-day routines. To keep all the balls in the air, remember the following:

- Have an overall view at all times. Even though as you do the work you concentrate on a particular step, each step should be part of a whole. The whole is the purpose of the project, what you are trying to accomplish. It will have been decided during the initial planning and setting up of various systems and always stays in the back of your mind to guide your efforts.

- Have a schedule on paper. During the initial planning you should work up a schedule that everyone agrees to. Even if you deviate from it, you will know by how much and what you have to do to catch up. Use it as a reference, especially during those beginning and middle stages, to orient yourself and get the project really moving.

- Have summary meetings prescheduled, on a regular basis. If a number of people are working on a project, such meetings are vital. They should be used to quickly review what has been done so far, to check the schedule, and to determine what still needs to be done at what pace. Such meetings also serve as a morale booster, reminding everyone that they are working together. If you are working on a project by yourself, also plan regularly scheduled times when you will appraise the progress of the work. If you don't do this,

it's too easy to forget various details and you will run
the risk of letting the project slip away from you.

- Assign one person to be "Information Central." That
person will be responsible for coordination—keeping
minutes, updating the schedule, knowing how the
different parts of the project are functioning. He or she
is someone to whom all the participants can automatically go either to find out specific information or to
ask who to go to for a decision.

Working with Deadlines

Deadlines keep us going. Without them, we tend to put off
things, succumbing to the belief that the work will get done
at some vague point in the future. And that is the purpose of
deadlines—they make the future specific. One can't hide
behind "when," "whenever," or "someday." They give us
something to aim for, turning our intentions and fantasies into
real plans.

Setting deadlines, whether for yourself or others, involves
a realistic appraisal of the task or project to be done. What is
realistic? It is taking into account *all* the factors that may play
a part: the work to be done, who is doing it, why it is being
done. It also means remembering to take into account how
people use time itself, from the need to fool themselves
regarding how time passes to how long they expect things to
take. In setting a deadline, make sure of the following:

- Always be specific. Don't rely on "soon." If it's to be
done tomorrow, set a time. If it's three months away,
set a day.
- Make sure the deadline is clear to all parties. Repeat it
if necessary.

- Don't be afraid of it. Being exact about a deadline doesn't mean you are being aggressive. It means you are being professional. If you really do want to soften it, say, "at noon," or "tomorrow morning," or "at the end of the month." But remember, the less exact you are, the more your deadline will be taken advantage of. Tomorrow morning all too easily turns into tomorrow afternoon. It's human nature.
- Write it down, wherever appropriate: your calendar, any memos you may be sending out, any minutes you may be keeping. All parties can use it later for reference.

Setting deadlines brings up the question of padding. Some people swear by it, others say it is an unnecessary game that is only played because of a lack of professionalism. Padding can cut two ways. Murphy's Law does seem universal, and everything usually takes longer than anticipated. If you devise a schedule with some extra "give" time, you will probably use it all up to bring out the work when you really want it out. However, if you get into a habit of padding, after a while, no one will be fooled, including yourself. You will know it is not the real deadline and will tend to ignore it.

And be careful of setting false deadlines to keep the pressure on someone. You may have legitimate reasons for setting an earlier due date for a certain task—if a person is chronically late, for example—and you can use the false date to prod them on. However, it can backfire if work is turned in late and there are no repercussions. You will lose credibility, and if you have to set a deadline for the same person at some future date, he or she will know that it is not real.

If you are working to meet a deadline that has been set for you, always take it seriously. Even if you happen to know that there is some leeway in the schedule, playing games with the deadline is dangerous. In the first place, there is always that straw that can break the camel's back: even if you have been chronically late and have never suffered repercussions, there is no guarantee that it will never happen. Perhaps others in your company who work on similar projects are also chronically late, and things may get so bad that eventually something will fall through the cracks. Or a new boss will step in. Or perhaps something unforeseen happens that changes all the rules. Claiming that being late never mattered before and that your work shouldn't be penalized won't get you very far. The damage will already have been done. Also, keeping to a schedule and then finding out that you had some extra time is at most annoying; at best, that extra time can be used for other work or improving that same project.

Emergencies and Crises

There is nothing like an emergency to destroy all your scheduling plans. Your priorities are turned upside-down in an instant. Events start happening so fast, time seems to rush by in a flash. Procedures fly out the window. You feel out of control. It is a prime set-up for wasted effort, frayed nerves and lost hours.

The prime solution for such a situation is getting back in control. The sooner you do this, the more effectively you will operate. That is the secret of "emergency management"— taking control of whatever happens before it takes control of you. If can do this, you are able to do your balancing act of meeting the needs of the emergency while taking care of the other things that would have filled in your time otherwise.

There is no predicting when an emergency will occur. You can't prepare for it—by its very definition it is something unforeseen. The chances of one occurring may increase if there is little organization in a company or if a system on a particular project has not been set up with good enough check points. Also, if you happen to be juggling too many things at once, the pressure will mount, the quality of work will drop, and mistakes will be made, all of which will lead to crises. The more deeply involved you are in that kind of working environment, the more vulnerable you are. It is yet another reason why good planning and good systems are so necessary in the workplace.

Assume you have just been hit with an emergency. What do you do? First of all, always tell yourself that you will not let it get the better of you. "Let" is the operative word here. You always have choices on how to respond in any given situation—even in an emergency. Keep reminding yourself of this power. It will help you in taking back control.

Also know that you can give an emergency back. When someone rushes in and tells you of a particular problem, it becomes yours. By bringing you the problem, the bearer has also brought a healthy new dose of tension into your life. Don't take it on without thinking it through—even if you must do your thinking instantaneously.

The moments right after an emergency is brought to your attention are always critical. Upon hearing the problem, you should:

- Listen to what is being said. Don't rush in with exclamations and ideas before you know the whole story. Listening will give you time to think and clarify the issues.
- Ask questions. It is another way to give yourself some breathing space and not take on the emergency unnecessarily. Determine what specifically is being asked of you. Try and find out why the emergency happened in the first place. Who needs what and when? The more

questions you can ask, the more time you will gain and
the more tension you will be able to avoid.

- Do a quick priority check to determine whether it is
  your place to deal with the problem. Weigh what you
  are doing and your remaining schedule for the day.
  Again, remember that it will be you who decides to
  change what may have been arranged previously. You
  are in charge, not the emergency.

- Be honest in your answer. If you do feel it is your place
  to deal with the problem, say so. If not, communicate
  that also, pointing out who the problem really "belongs" to. (Note that in pointing this out, you are
  being helpful, not passing the buck. If you genuinely
  feel that you want to help even though it's not your
  area of concern, by all means do so. It is when you
  make a habit of taking on everyone else's problems that
  something is wrong.)

- Take the action needed immediately. If the problem is
  yours, do whatever has to be done to take care of
  matters. If it is not and you have said so, make a polite
  but firm show of getting back to whatever you were
  doing previously: say you have to get back to your
  work, look down at your desk, pick up the telephone.
  Your message will be conveyed instantly.

Notice the overall effect of the above guidelines. You are
acting on the problem instead of reacting. You have called the
shots, instead of passively letting someone tell you what to do.
This doesn't mean you are slow to respond or are not
cooperating. All of the above calculations are done as soon as
the problem is communicated to you. Any seconds you lose in
organizing your thoughts or preparing your response are
nothing compared to the time you might lose in not taking
appropriate action, whether you deal with the problem or give
it back to someone else.

A word about working under pressure. You may put off things constantly, not getting to them until absolutely necessary, telling yourself that it is okay, that you work best that way. Don't fool yourself, however. You may still get things done, even on time, but your work will not be as good as it could be. No one really works best under pressure. Pressure is a false motivating tool that you use because you can't motivate yourself in any other way. Coping with pressure takes energy. You may feel uplifted by it, but you are using your own energy to create that feeling. If the task were spread out over a greater period of time, that energy could be used on more careful work, not on coping with the pressure.

Spare Moments

The opposite of the emergency is the small, spare moment when nothing of value seems to be getting done. It is the down time between big projects or the minute you take to rest in your chair during periods of hectic activity. These spare moments don't just happen. Whether consciously or not, you create them when you feel they are necessary, when your body tells you it needs to regenerate itself, when your psyche demands a break, too.

Can you schedule such moments? Should you use them for something other than doing absolutely nothing? Don't you run the risk of becoming an automaton if your every moment is filled up with some activity or other? These are the questions that come up when talk turns to making good use of the spare moments that are part of the natural cycle of every working day. And well they should. As the media makes the world seem smaller day by day, as technology makes communication instant, we often feel as though we are operating on fast forward. Those spare minutes become very precious—sometimes the only moments of sanity we experience all day. Doing nothing seems like the best thing in the world, and the last thing we want to do is turn such moments into something productive.

The question is not one of barring yourself from ever resting, however. No matter how pressurized the situation or how zealous you may be about getting things done, there will be times when your body says enough. And you will have to listen. If you don't, or if you let yourself get to the brink too often, all your lost moments of relaxation may be given back to you in the form of extended sick leave. Even during the fairly average day—if there is such a thing—you will take moments to socialize, to daydream, or break your rhythm in a hundred different ways. These breaks will happen because they should happen.

What is at issue is the way these breaks are used. Sometimes, instead of rest, what you are really looking for is distraction. You're not tired, you just want a change of pace. If you get into the habit of always doing the same thing during such spare moments, you are wasting the energy you do have. Try to notice the difference, so you can start using those spare moments well. In that sense you can schedule them—you can make a conscious decision that you will use such moments to do things that you want to do anyway, but just "can't find the time."

And what should those things be? They should be activities that, as much as possible, are opposite to what you have been doing. Involving yourself with something totally different is the key. If you have been concentrating for a long time, perform small tasks that can be done quickly, such as some filing or going through odds and ends. If you have been working alone, return some phone calls or take care of work that involves seeing another person. On the other hand, if you have been in meetings or on the phone all day, go through some of those magazines or paperwork that has piled up on your desk. The point is to take those numerous little tasks that have been accumulating and—instead of looking at them as one big project with many components—breaking it all up and doing one thing at time when the opportunity presents itself. Like a stack of magazines on a desk, such tasks will seem much less intimidating when done separately as opposed to being tackled at once. You will not only have accomplished something by doing them, you will reenergize yourself to boot.

Using Your Calendar

Your calendar is your primary scheduling tool. Whether you use a pocket variety, a desk calendar, or some other reminder, there should be one place where you write down what you have to do. A calendar is where your priorities and the minutes of your day or the days of your month come together. Once you have written something down, a calendar allows you to forget it so you don't waste energy to keep it "on the back burner." When the appropriate times comes, it will be the calendar that will remind you what to do.

A calendar also allows you to see your day or your week or month as a whole. At a quick glance you have an overview of what you plan to be doing during any given period of time. This should help you in further planning as you decide whether to "fit something in" or postpone it till a later date.

Keeping these two purposes of a calendar in mind—it serves as an automatic reminder and it gives you an overview—should guide you as you work with it to schedule your time. In the first place, it should always be accessible to you. If you have a job that involves traveling or being out of the office often, you will want a calendar that you can take with you wherever you go. A desk calendar will provide more room for writing things down, but it won't be as accessible. Even if you don't spend much time outside the office, there may be times in the evenings or during weekends when you remember something significant. Having your calendar with you will save you from writing it down on a scrap piece of paper, which can more easily be lost, or writing it down a second time when you get to work.

The calendar will serve as an automatic reminder only if you take advantage of it. You will have to make it a point to go over it on a steady basis to see how you have scheduled yourself. Besides going over it day by day, make a point of checking it week by week so you get that overall picture of what's coming up and can make plans early enough for something that may have slipped your mind. (And things will slip your mind! Not the important conference or due date for the yearly report that you are working on, but the smaller things that don't seem crucial yet turn out to be when you forget to plan for them: a lunch date with a regular client for whom you have to look up some information, scheduling to discuss a problem of work flow that may be occurring between you and a coworker or another department, even bringing something from home to the office on a particular day.) Any preparation for such things may done quickly—or it may not. Leaving it to chance and having to do it under pressure is not good time management. Periodically checking your calendar will cut down on sloppy work or needless rushing around.

When you do write down something in your calendar, don't be too brief or too cryptic. It is easy to do this, especially when you are having a stressful day. You may be tempted to use initials in making a lunch date, for example. Or abbreviate words or names. But imagine yourself a week or a month from now. Will those initials or abbreviations mean something? Watch out for this tendency—writing it out a little more clearly or fully can save you time and embarrassment in the long run.

And watch out for that age-old problem of overbooking yourself. This happens when we don't take into consideration all those seemingly inconsequential details—our energy level, the unforeseen details, the messiness of every working day—that we often don't want to acknowledge. On paper, three weeks or two months from now, everything looks possible and scheduling three or four meetings in one day may seem perfectly fine. But it won't be fine when you actually get to that day and start attending those meetings, as well as coping with everything else that is happening. Only then will you realize you have been unrealistic in scheduling your time. Always, put yourself in that future time period to decide whether your scheduling makes sense.

7

Time and the Office Routine: Organizing the Basics

It is called the office routine because that's exactly what it is: a series of tasks that you and millions of other office workers do on a continual basis. They are the basic tools of business—filing, correspondence, the telephone—and they don't change greatly from day to day, if at all. You learned how to do them at your first job and chances are you are still doing many of them, no matter how high up the ladder you have moved. Chances are also high, however, that you have never thought of them in relation to time. This chapter will point you in that direction. Perhaps you can perform some of those tasks a little differently or at a different hour. Perhaps you can dispense with some of them or take others on to good effect. Although they don't seem like much when looked at individually, the seconds and minutes you may save do add up.

Your greatest help in saving time on these tasks is organization. Although in some respects organization has become a dirty word implying rigidity, even the most seemingly disorganized person has set up certain routines or procedures. When reacting against any forced organization, what he or she is saying is, "Don't foist your organization onto me. I have my own way of doing things—no matter how crazy it may seem to you." Though such a person is right, he or she overlooks the fact that in some respects organization implies the same things for everybody.

Being organized is having a system for whatever task you may be doing. This system interacts with other systems for other tasks, which becomes your overall method of working. In Chapter Four we looked at the importance of having systems in general, why we have them, how they help in working with others in the company. This chapter will look at systems on a small scale—think of them as systems for your own desk or office. They are time-saving tips that you can incorporate into your daily routine. They may also lead you to develop systems of your own. In either case, you may be surprised at how much time you "find" to spend on other things.

In Chapter Four we also discussed the importance of doing things automatically, which is a result of having systems. This ability to do things without thinking, almost reflexively, is at its most useful with routine tasks, simply because there are so many and we do them so often. Doing things automatically also cuts down on stress—you won't be kicking yourself that you can't find that memo quickly enough when time is of the essence.

It is this automatic ability to do things that the disorganized person prides himself on. "See," he may be saying during those same times of stress. "Even though my desk looks disorganized, I know exactly where everything is. I found that memo as quickly as an organized person would." In many cases this may be true. The disorganized person is priding himself on keeping track of all the clutter in his mind. But the energy used for keeping that organization in his head could be used for other things. And he is leaving things to chance. When the energy level isn't quite up to snuff, or when he is distracted, or when the pressure mounts, what usually seems automatic can suddenly take frustratingly long minutes to accomplish. At that point, he is much worse off than someone who has allowed organization to free his energy for the tasks at hand.

Your Office and Desk

Knowing where things are and having access to that information immediately is the purpose behind organizing your working environment. How you set up your desk or office doesn't matter—it is being able to get to things that matters. If everything looks orderly and yet you don't remember where certain files or memos are, you are not really organized. The same rule holds true for the person who seems like a slob—if he or she knows exactly where to find everything (and we are not taking into consideration the problems discussed above) then there is some organization present. Whenever you set out to organize the space you work in—whether you're taking over a new position or merely doing "spring cleaning," that is your rule of thumb: being able to get to things with the minimum amount of time and effort.

If you are taking over a new space, keep in mind the following:

- Get to know what's there first. Look through the files in the desk, see what's on the shelves of the office, look through the cabinets—no matter how daunting they seem! Make this task a priority and schedule an hour for it each day. Do this until the space becomes yours, so to speak—until you feel comfortable with it and know the basics of what has been stored where.

- Watch the flow of work. See what comes in and where any information needed to complete the work—memos, files, lists—is kept. This linking of incoming work with what is stored in your office or desk is important. The more you do this the faster you will feel comfortable with the space.

- Take your duties into account. As far as you know, have there been any duties added to the position you have taken over? Have any duties been taken away? Consider the files you need to complete the duties. You may have to do some shifting around, getting rid of some files and adding others.

When you feel comfortable with your work and the location of materials you are to work with, you are ready to organize your space. You want to have those files closest to you that you use most often. If you have to look up something five times a day, you don't want to go down the hall to do it. Another consideration is complexity of the task or the bulk of certain files. You may do a certain task a little less often, but it involves using big files or several of them at once. You would want to keep these files close by also, to minimize on the time and effort for dragging the files out. Some tasks will be more sensitive than others—certain files may contain confidential information or material that should only be seen by you or one or two others. You want these files close by, preferably under lock and key. Since you will have only a set amount of space to work with, you won't be able to have everything at your fingertips. Always consider the different factors—frequency, complexity, confidentiality—when you are making your decisions in how to set yourself up.

Your desk top is your most frequently used work area. As such, you want to feel at home with it. For most people, that means the bulk of the desk is clear of paperwork and clutter. A messy desk top not only makes it harder to find things, but also looks more daunting. The same amount of work arranged neatly will look much more accessible than work scattered all over the place. The rest of the desktop should be reserved for frequently used files and office equipment. If your desk is big enough, you will also want to have an in-box and out-box on it. If your desk is too small, have the in/out boxes someplace nearby—but clearly marked and distinctly separate from your other work. You want to get to your in/out boxes quickly, but you also want to avoid confusion for people dropping off things or picking things up from you.

As far as clutter is concerned, even if you are one of those people who thinks that a messy desk is a sign of genius, as the saying goes, you have to remember the impression it gives others: things are out of control, you have too much work, you don't care, you are stressed out. Be careful of trying to hide behind that scenario. Even if someone considers that mess on your desk a sign of how busy and hardworking you are, it still does not build much confidence in you, no matter how sorry someone may feel for your plight. Rightly or wrongly, they associate some problem with the messiness of your surroundings.

If you are one of those people who cannot conceive of having everything put away out of sight in drawers or cabinets, consider putting your work into piles on top of your desk or on shelves or cabinets nearby. Sort the piles by the types of work they represent or the urgency with which the work must get done, as always, keeping the most urgent closest to you. After a while, you will know, just by glancing at a pile, how much of what kind of work you have left to do. It will save you precious seconds in calculating what to take on next.

The Telephone

The telephone is yet another example of an invention that was created to save time, but which more often than not seems to cause the opposite effect. "If only the phone would stop ringing, I'd get so much done!"—how often have we heard that refrain? Why does the ringing of the phone seem so insidious? Why are there so many jokes about cutting the wires and breaking the system? What is it about this contraption that makes many people hate it so much and consider it to be their greatest time waster of all? Looking at some of these issues and sorting them out will help us sort out our own views of the telephone and enable us to use it for saving rather than wasting time.

Perhaps most importantly the phone is a symbol of control—or our lack of it. There we are, all set to work on project A with project B waiting in the wings if we finish A—and the phone rings. We pray that the interruption will be short, that the caller a) won't be longwinded, b) won't give us more work, c) won't ask too many questions, d) won't be our boss demanding that we come to her office. The point is we don't know—we can only pray.

There is also an intrusiveness about the telephone. We have created our private little world for the moment, are working away conscientiously—often after a good dose of procrastination—and there's that ring, bringing us back to reality.

Underlying both of these issues is a feeling of passivity. The more powerless we feel—that we have to carry out the caller's request no matter what time demands it may place on us—the more we tend to resent the phone's interruptions. It goes back to the belief we discussed earlier, that someone else's time is more valuable than our own.

Thinking of the phone as an instrument that we control for our benefit, instead of something that is there for everyone else's benefit, is the first step in ending this love-hate relationship. Good screening of calls is a must. If you have an assistant or secretary, half your battle is won already. However, setting good, reasonable ground rules is the other half. In setting down the guidelines, watch out for the following:

- Make sure your assistant knows where you are throughout the day.
- Be in agreement on when you can't be disturbed.
- Tell your assistant who, if anyone, should get special treatment. It's something we often don't like to address because we don't want to admit that anyone gets special treatment. However, reality is different. (Especially watch out for this with any temporary personnel who may be working for you. If the president or CEO is used to calling everybody and getting through immediately, you don't want your temp to say, "Larry who?" or "Mary . . . can you please spell your last name?" It can be embarrassing, if not worse.)
- Review frequently asked questions that callers may have of you and formulate standard answers that should be given.
- Help your assistant with the difficult callers. It doesn't mean you have to pick up the call (although at times it cannot be avoided). But if your assistant comes to you bewildered in the middle of a difficult call, don't let your irritation with the caller be transferred onto your assistant. Help out with what to say. The time you take will be much appreciated.

- Be careful with lying—your assistant will learn to do it
  soon enough anyway. All the standards, "He's tied up
  at the moment," "She's in a meeting," "He just
  stepped out," work fine—as long as your assistant
  doesn't step away and you pick up the next call which
  happens to be from the same irate person. As often
  happens with lying, you may get the opposite of what
  you were hoping for and end up spending more time
  explaining yourself.

If you don't have an assistant, you will have to do the
screening yourself. Technological advances such as voice mail
help with taking messages when you aren't there. If you are
there, however, you will have to answer the calls—leaving a
ringing telephone unanswered is very unprofessional and is not
done. If you feel the interruption has come at a bad time—if
you are in a meeting with someone, for example—don't be
afraid to say so. Politely explain the circumstances and ask for
the best time to call the person back. If it's someone
longwinded who is calling, after the initial polite exchanges,
try to steer them to the point of their call. "Is this the problem
you called me about?" or "If I understand you correctly, you
want/need/hope that. . . ." or something similar with which
you can cut in at an appropriate time.

When someone calls with a request that entails a little bit
of work on your part, you have two choices: you can leave them
on hold while you do whatever is needed, or you can tell them
you will call them back. Doing the work while someone is on
hold means that you do the work right there and then and that
you don't have to worry about it later. Telling someone you
will call back usually means that the work will take a bit
longer—even if it's the same task—because without someone
waiting on the other end, you have less pressure on you.

If you possibly can, urge those responsible to purchase

speaker phones or the latest technology that leaves your hands free while you're on the phone. Being able to get up and retrieve a file while you're talking or being able to concentrate on another task if you happen to be on hold for any length of time is a great time saver. Cradling the receiver between your ear and your shoulder is not quite the same thing: Your mind is on your shoulder and the receiver more than anywhere else. And it is not exactly comfortable.

And remember, when you are answering a call always have scrap paper and pencil handy—not only to write down a name and phone number, but also to jot down bits of information as you are talking. It will help you if you are trying to relay a message to someone else; and more importantly, if the call is for you, it will help you in your work later on—you will have the information right there and may save yourself some searching and calling back.

Returning phone calls can seem even more time consuming—especially if you've been away from your desk and come back to find it covered with phone messages. Your first step should be to glance through them to prioritize and determine which need to be acted on immediately, and which can wait. And prioritize carefully—you are dealing with that old human need for instant gratification! Despite what the messages say, many of the callers will survive if you don't call back right away. Choose the time to do so accordingly.

Return some of the lower-priority calls during those spare moments between bigger projects. They will provide a break in your rhythm, and you will be getting work done at the same time. If you have to call someone longwinded back, try to do so a bit before lunch, before leaving for the day, or a short while before you know you will have to end the call. It will force you to keep the conversation at a reasonable length.

Then there is the problem—some people make it a game—of telephone tag. The game players don't mind the constant back-and-forth of exchanging phone messages without actually talking to each other. To them, the main thing is that both parties have shown enough courtesy to return the other's call. That is important—despite enough examples to the contrary, business is run on courtesy, not on rudeness. However, if it is important for you to get beyond courtesy to save time and actually share information—leave a specific hour when you can be reached and make sure you are available when you said you would be. If you are talking to someone's secretary or assistant, try to find out from them what the call may have been about and pass on any information you need to. It may save you a repeat call.

Finally, never dispense with initial, polite exchanges with those on the other end, whether you are calling or they are calling you. You can always manage a polite, "Hello," and a quick sentence or two no matter how pressured you may feel. If you launch into your problems or request immediately, it will be considered rude. If you are under great time pressure, say so politely but firmly so the caller will know why you are being abrupt.

Writing and Reading

In many ways, modern technology, especially the telephone, has replaced writing as the primary means of communication. Talking on the telephone is much quicker than writing a memo or a letter. Our tendency is to pick up the phone to do business instead of turning to the typewriter or word processing equipment. The phone is certainly faster and more efficient, but is it always more effective? Before you dismiss writing that memo or letter, think of the long-range, overall benefits a written document may serve. Consider the following, especially if the matter at hand is complex, involving many people, components, or a longer time frame:

- You have time to think. Writing something down allows you to collect your thoughts and put them down in a more organized way. Reading something allows for a more organized response.

- Because something written tends to be more organized, problems and procedures can be spelled out more clearly.

- A written document gives you an overall picture. Whether the document entails a small aspect of a larger problem or the entire problem, the time it takes to write something down puts the matter in better perspective.

- You can use the memo or letter as a point of reference in the future. This is where the time saving comes in most handily. Instead of scrambling around for information, trying to remember exactly what you discussed with your client six months ago, you have it there in writing.

Implied in the above statements is the expectation that the writing itself will be clear and organized. Because time is of the essence in the modern business world, many people have dismissed writing because they associate it with verbosity, confusion, and the time wasted to decipher anything written. Memos are the most common form of written communication in the office. In writing them, always follow the guidelines below:

- be brief (no more than a page, hopefully less)
- get to the point
- use bullets and underlining for emphasis
- make clear what you expect the reader to do

- make sure the routing is clear
- choose positives over double negatives
- choose the active voice over the passive ("I noticed," rather than "It has come to my attention")

By definition a letter will be more formal and will probably contain fewer breaks, bullets, and elements designed to get the reader's attention; but the same rules of clarity and conciseness should be followed.

If you receive a memo and the response required of you is short, you should be able to write it on the memo itself and send it back. It will not only save you the time in typing a new memo, the entire exchange will be on one piece of paper.

In writing anything, watch those revisions. While you want to go over something to make sure there are no misspellings or errors, don't fall into perfectionism. If you want to, you can always think of more to say or a better way to write it; deciding to be more polite, or more forceful. If you are really unsure of yourself, put it down for an hour or two and do other work. Then come back to it and see how it reads. With this fresh perspective you'll be able to clarify problems much more quickly; more often than not, you'll find that what you have written is totally acceptable.

Reading the memos and letters you receive tests your ability to pick out necessary information. If the writer has been helpful in emphasizing the main points clearly, you should have little problem with this. If not, you will have to read more closely. Teach yourself to skim effectively. Good skimming is particularly helpful in reading longer reports as well as magazines and newspapers that cross your desk. It's the age-old problem: You want to know what's happening in your company and in your industry, but you never feel there's enough time to read. Skimming helps. Run your eye down the page and look for specific words and phrases that catch your interest. If you feel that closer reading is appropriate, you can slow down.

If you have an assistant and are particularly pressed for time, give them whatever needs to be read and ask for a report or capsule review. In addition to saving you some time, they will be able to learn something and practice their own writing skills.

And don't let that pile of magazines and newspapers get too high. The higher the pile gets the more apt you are to lose interest in whatever was inside those magazines or newspapers that made them appear worth keeping in the first place. Either too much time has passed or you are now concentrating on other things. Read them one at time—perhaps during those spare moments or on your commute to and from work—and then throw them away or pass them on. Unread, they only represent more clutter.

Filing, Sorting Your In-Box
Dictating, Xeroxing

Filing. You may be lucky and have a super secretary who does everything for you. Stories abound of executives who have retired or left their jobs and have suddenly found they don't know their way around the post office or a xerox machine. However, if you're like most mortals, you are still doing some of these tasks, whether you have someone to assist you in your work or not. Don't just take each task for granted. You can probably save some time on them all.

We have already discussed the location of files in your office. As far as the files themselves are concerned, don't be afraid of color coding. Although it may sound like something too trivial to bother with, it can save you time. If you have an array of files in a drawer or on a shelf and are looking for a particular file, differences in color can automatically lead your eye to where you need to look. If you need a folder containing invoices, for example, and that folder is green, you won't have to spend time reading the labels of manila-colored folders, or worse, looking through the folders themselves.

Organizing files to represent the *type* of work is preferable to filing by *urgency* of the work. Things that really have to be done immediately can be separated out, but if you start crossfiling things, you usually end up just creating extra paperwork for yourself. Besides, once you have become comfortable with a job, you can immediately associate the type of work with its urgency. Use a "To Do" List instead of creating yet another file.

Sorting Your In-Box. It is a bit unreasonable to try and live up to the maxim that every piece of paper should only cross your desk once. The word *unnecessarily* should be added to that maxim. When you go through your in-box sorting mail and other paperwork, you want to make the appropriate decision what to do with it—and then not make that same decision again. In essence, you want to know whether the piece of paper in your hand should be:

- responded to immediately
- represents work to be done later
- belongs in the wastebasket
- should be read and then filed away

Do what needs to be done and then forget that piece of paper. If it is something that you have set aside to be done in the future, that's fine. When you pick up the piece of paper again, you should be ready to do the work it represents. Putting it off again shouldn't be necessary—that decision was made earlier.

Dictating. Dictating should save you time—but only if you don't have to spell out difficult words, think of the correct punctuation, or construct each sentence carefully. To use dictation to maximum efficiency try to have your assistant take on this work from the very beginning. It will be good training, and also save time for you.

This doesn't mean, of course, that you should flaunt your executive status and make life difficult for the assistant. You can help by first giving the overall purpose of the letter or memo you want written, mention the specific points you want to make, perhaps including specific phrases or references, and let it go at that. The more time passes the more your assistant should be able to write for you, leaving you free for other tasks.

If you are the assistant being asked to write something, refer to an example of a letter or memo done on a similar topic or written to the same person. In referring to what was done previously, pay attention to its tone and look for phrases and constructions that you can use until you feel more at ease doing the correspondence on your own.

Photocopying. Xeroxing—the biggest heachache, the most frustrating time-waster, the task we most want to leave for those lowest on the totem pole and never think about.

Xeroxing seems to cause more problems than it solves because the expectations are so great. Whatever the manuscript, report, memo, document, letter, we can always make as many copies as needed—or so we think. Everybody also thinks the same way, and asks us for a copy. We gladly oblige. But then the machine breaks down, our assistant is sick, there is a long line at the one machine that works, and we end up feeling frustrated.

At the same time, however, having a copy is a necessary safety net. Nothing is as embarrassing as losing that important piece of paper. It's better—much better—to be safe than sorry. How do we deal with this dilemma?

It's not easy. You can help yourself by looking realistically at those expectations to determine whether the extra copies are really warranted. Is everybody going to use the document at the same time? If one person or department will have need of it before another, perhaps they can share it. If people aren't happy with this arrangement, worrying about unexpected delays or developments, assure them they can come back to you for more xeroxes in the future.

If you know something will be requested by others, try to make copies *before* others ask you for them. You won't have to do the xeroxing under so much pressure and may be able to use your spare moments for the task. If time is not of the essence, try to route documents and memos instead of copying them. And always make one copy for yourself, to be kept nearby, while the original is circulating or being copied en masse. If it is lost, you have yours as a backup.

Vacation

Have you ever sworn off vacations because of the extra work you had to do before leaving and on coming back? While a certain amount of extra time and effort before and after vacation is to be expected, most of it can be scaled down if you just do some advance planning.

In the first place, in scheduling days off, remember that as time goes on, proportionately less and less work will find its way onto your desk. That is, if you are away for two days, for example, you often come back to a very messy looking desk. But if you are away two weeks—ten days—your desk will not be five times as messy when you come back. After those initial few days, your coworkers become more used to your absence, and either take care of work themselves or resolve to wait until you get back.

Informing coworkers and clients that you will be away is important—they may need your input for something—but it presents problems also—you don't want everyone lining up outside your door before you go away. Some of the lining up will be unavoidable—but you can also regulate it to an extent. Be judicious in who you tell you are leaving and don't do it all at the last minute.

Of course, you don't want twenty people waiting for you at 9 A.M. on the morning of your return, either. That is where advance planning comes in. Before leaving, go over the work to be done in your absence and see what will need your input. Take care of what you can, and more importantly, make sure there will be someone who can make decisions in your absence. If you have good systems in place, there should be such a person available. It may not save you from some early and late hours of catching up, but it may prevent your needing a vacation from your vacation.

8

Time and Your Coworkers: Delegating and Working Together

If you have one or more than one person working for you, knowing how to delegate well can be your biggest time saver. Delegating doesn't mean you are passing the buck and giving your work to someone else; rather, it means knowing how to tell the difference between what is best done by you and what should be passed on to an assistant. It consists of three parts:

- deciding what work you will delegate
- presenting the work to your subordinate
- setting up control points

In deciding on the work that you will pass on, you will have to make a realistic appraisal of the work itself, your subordinate's capabilities, and the value of your own time. In going over your responsibilities, ask yourself which ones lend themselves best to being given away. First of all, consider any day-to-day tasks you have. Anything that is routine is fairly easily given over to an assistant. You explain it once or twice, perhaps answer a few questions afterwards, do a quick check of the work the first few times, and if all has gone well you can let the responsibility for the work rest on your assistant's shoulders.

However, you also want your assistant to learn and grow, so you want to enlist help on bigger, one-of-a-kind projects, too. But that entails the very real problem of your explaining something that is unfamiliar, perhaps complex, and will not be done very often, if ever again. There is more than enough reason to believe that you will save time—and mistakes—by doing this kind of work yourself. It is a legitimate concern, and doing it well is the key to good delegating.

To get around this problem, first see if you can break down the project into smaller parts—parts that are self-contained and which may be similar to work your assistant is already doing. Also, consider which aspects of the project your assistant may use in future work. Even if the project itself is never repeated, perhaps portions of it, or something similar, will be. And think about any special interests or areas of expertise your assistant may have shown in the past. Perhaps some aspects of the project will dovetail nicely with those concerns.

You will also want to weigh your assistant's strengths and weaknesses against the work itself. Pick aspects of the project that draw on strengths rather than weaknesses. Or, depending on your own time pressures, you may feel it important to have your assistant improve certain skills. You can assign aspects of the project that give those skills a good workout. In that case, you will have to be prepared for mistakes. Even if the work is easy, however, you will have to ask yourself what you will do if your assistant does not perform well. What control points will you set up for the work? How much time will you have to help in correcting any problems? Note the word "help." You don't want to take the work back, which will be demoralizing to your assistant. If you can at all do so, devote time to pointing out problem areas, asking specific questions, guiding rather than directing your assistant through to completion of the work. This may be more work than you bargained for, and you have to be prepared for it.

In all of this, of course, you can't forget your own time. How pressured are you? How much of a priority is this particular job? Would you enjoy doing it yourself? Or are you just keeping it because you are afraid your assistant will make a mess of it?

Once you have decided on the work, you will need to explain what you want done. In presenting any work, always remember that you want to be supportive rather than intimidating. Being intimidating may get you results in the short run, but it will not be conductive to a good working relationship, let alone improving your assistant's learning curve. In order to present the work as effectively—and time consciously—as possible, keep in mind the following:

- give a quick overview of the purpose of the entire project
- explain how your assistant's part fits in
- briefly review what you expect your assistant to do
- use examples to illustrate the work
- give a quick summary
- ask if your assistant has any questions
- set appropriate control points

Setting intelligent control points will also save you time and effort. Once you have presented the work to your assistant, you want to be able to forget about it so you can concentrate on other tasks. The checkpoints should be automatic triggers— that is, they should require no effort from you. You can base them on:

- a particular schedule (agree ahead of time when you and your assistant will go over the work)
- specific portions of the work being completed
- particular problems (your assistant will come to you for help if certain problems come up)

The important consideration is to set up the control points in advance. Organizing them in one manner or another takes the burden off your shoulders because you don't have to keep a constant eye out for the progress of the work. You know you will get to see the work on the schedule you have arranged with your assistant and will be able to resolve problems then.

It's always a trade-off. Delegating takes time in the beginning: deciding on the work, assigning it, reviewing it. The time you hope to save is in the future; if you have delegated well, the trade-off will be worth it.

Meetings

Nothing can eat away at your time like meetings. At a meeting, you usually spend only a small percentage of your time focused directly on your work. The rest of the time is spent on everybody else's work. This is not all bad, of course. The purpose of a meeting is to bring together a group of people to share information. A well-run meeting gives you an overview of what's happening and a chance to share thoughts with your coworkers—and hopefully, get something accomplished. It can be a good learning experience. However, the learning curve can drop sharply if the meeting goes on too long or covers the same ground that has been covered before. Furthermore, this problem is hard to control; what is a learning experience for one person may be old news for someone else. Everybody can't be accommodated, and often, the best that can be hoped for is a decent consensus: an agreement on a good length for the meeting and on what is discussed, so that the topics address at least the basic concerns of the participants.

Regularly scheduled meetings present a particular problem in this regard. Meetings on a regular basis are needed to keep a company going—to give the participants a chance to gauge the progress of work and to plan for the future. However, since many topics discussed are strictly routine, the chances are great for repeating what was said the week or the month before. As a participant at such meetings, you are tempted to skip one or "phone in" whatever you have to say. But the "Catch-22" is that your presence is needed—something new *may* come up, your input *may* be needed, you *may* learn of a procedure that has a direct bearing on your job. And what's more, everybody is in the same position—not showing up is disrespectful of everybody's time.

If you participate in regularly scheduled meetings, there are things you can do to cut down on wasted time. You'll never be totally successful, and you are bound to feel frustrated on some occasions, but if you pay careful attention to it, the wasted time will feel minimal.

- Do an inventory of the meetings you attend regularly. Are there any that feel particularly wasteful of your time? If so, is your participation mandatory? Raise the issue with your boss and see what the response is. In doing so, consider how much you contribute to each meeting and how much you take away from it.

- Think of ways you can make improvements in meetings you have to attend. Be innovative. Perhaps you can stay only for the first half or come later. Or perhaps a designated person can call you when your presence is needed. Also note the agenda. Perhaps the topics discussed can be switched around and grouped together so that you and others can make better use of your time.

- When you are giving presentations at meetings or bringing up topics for discussion, be considerate of everybody's time. Be brief, clear, and stick to the facts. If you want to bring up a particular problem, make sure it's in keeping with what is being discussed. If you are repeating information given before, don't say the same thing. Informing everybody that there has been no change or giving a quick summary is adequate enough.

- Be prepared. You don't want to be looking through your notes, hemming and hawing, while everybody impatiently waits for you to get on with it. Whether someone has done their homework or not is always very apparent at meetings.

- Be careful about complaining. Unless the meeting has been called for everyone to specifically discuss problems, no one wants to hear you complaining. Nothing seems like a bigger waste of time.

- Also be careful of doing something else when the meeting turns to concerns that don't interest you. You can jot down unfinished business that comes to your mind or make a quick list of things to do, but don't attempt anything that requires any real concentration. As hard as it may be, you are there to concentrate on what's happening at the meeting. It is embarrassing to be caught not paying attention; you never know when that "Catch-22" may come at you head on and your opinion is solicited.

- It is acceptable to leave before the meeting is over—if you have informed whoever is running the meeting of this at the beginning. Not doing so is considered rude because it seems as though you are leaving because you are suddenly uninterested. You would expect others to treat you the same way.

　　If you are running a meeting, you have added responsibilities. By virtue of your position you are the main timekeeper. Everyone defers to you and your judgment. It is up to you to decide when the meeting is veering off-course.

- In scheduling the meeting, try to plan for it to last no more than an hour to an hour and a half. After that, attention levels drop considerably. If the meeting must be longer, institute breaks every hour or so.

- In planning the meeting, also watch for how many people will be attending. If necessary, investigate who does what and choose your participants in keeping with the main purpose of the meeting. Try to pare down your list—the more people that attend, the longer things will take.

- Have an agenda. Make a list of what you want discussed. Clearly state the purpose of the meeting at the beginning and what you hope to accomplish. This should help keep the participants on track.

- Keep things moving. Don't let people get too bogged down in details or secondary concerns. If details are discussed, make sure they are part of the overall plan for the meeting. For example, if participants start discussing who does what on a particular project, this is quite all right if the meeting has been called to solve a problem in the work flow or resolve a gap in communication. If the meeting has been called to go over the progress of various projects, another meeting may be needed for specific problems.

- Watch out when opinions expressed get too personal or specific. People with axes to grind often see meetings as a good occasion to vent their feelings. Meetings, however, are not good places to discuss an individual's problems; they are for the group as a whole, and only problems that have direct bearing on the agenda should be considered.

- Don't be too quick to call another meeting. Some problems are better served by having someone first write up a memo or report that can be circulated to the appropriate people. If necessary, a meeting may be called then.

Interruptions

The phone isn't the only cause of interruptions at work. Your coworkers and clients, assistants and bosses may do more than their fair share of popping by your desk or office unexpectedly. While you want to keep the interruptions manageable, you also have to remember that a company is a social organization—a certain number of interruptions will be inevitable. How you negotiate the fine line between doing your work and responding to your coworkers' needs is the test of good "interruption management." The better you do it, the better you will feel about the use of your time.

A constant source of interruption may be your assistant or secretary, who keeps popping his or her head in to ask questions, solicit advice, or give you information. Before you angrily turn your assistant away, think of the working arrangement you have set up. Perhaps you have solicited the interruptions yourself by the informality of your work habits, or your own interruptions. To solve this problem, set up more structure to your day. Inform your assistant when you don't want to be disturbed. And leave her alone accordingly. Also, institute a ten- or fifteen-minute meeting with her every day to go over any matters that need your input. Getting together every day keeps the meetings short and current; you won't be discussing something that should have been taken care of a week before.

Coworkers are another big source of interruptions. If you hear the line, "Have you got a minute?" watch out. The minute can easily turn into twenty—if you let it. When someone comes up to your desk or pops their head into your office with a request for your time, the following questions should run through you mind almost instantaneously:

- is the request legitimate (am I the person to come to)?
- how much time will this take?
- can someone else deal with this besides me?
- what does my schedule look like right now?

If you think the request is legitimate and can be done quickly, it's best to get it over with so that you don't have yet another task waiting for you. If it's legitimate but you feel you don't have the time for it at present, write down the request and tell the person you will get back to them when you can. If you're really pressed for time and will be for the near future, suggest someone else who can take care of the matter.

Very often, however, it's not that simple. The person

dropping by may be: a windbag, a gossip, a complainer, a friend needing to socialize. They ignore any signs that you are busy and plop themselves down for a good long stay. In the first place, you have to make sure that you aren't taken in by the gossip or socializing. As busy as you are, you may enjoy listening to the person and unconsciously put out signals that you'd much rather talk to them than do your work. Once you have made your decision to get them to leave, you can do various things. Stand up at your desk; that is a signal for most people that a conversation is over. If someone needs a stronger hint, you can actually leave your desk or office, with an excuse that you have to go to the bathroom or see someone upstairs. If it's a recurring problem and you want to avoid someone who has made a habit of coming by to waste time, develop a game plan with a sympathetic assistant or colleague. Have someone call you when they see the person by your desk, informing you that you are needed in another part of the office or that your boss is calling you.

If it's a boss who is doing the interrupting, it may be because they have become used to operating that way. Although you have to tread carefully, you still have options. If they call or pop by, and you really feel something else is a greater priority, politely mention it and *ask* if it's okay to carry out the request later. You have rightly put the ball in their court and have asked them to make the decision. Implicit in this notion is the fact that you agree to whatever they decide.

In the end, if you really need to do serious work and can absolutely brook no interruptions, you have only two options: closing the door to your office—if you have one—or going to hide someplace where you can't be found. The first option will only work if you have a trusty assistant who knows how to screen your calls well and steer people away from your door. Without an office, your only real option is to do the work someplace else. If it's a recurring problem, you should talk to your boss about it. Bring up the possibility of changing your duties or moving your work station to another area.

Saying No

Saying no is a great time saver. If you are in the habit of constantly agreeing with everything everyone says or being the one to do favors and carry out requests, look at your reasons for doing so carefully. Very often, being agreeable covers up a sense of insecurity: You will take on the work to cover up the fact that you don't do a good enough job as it is or you think badly of yourself in some other respect. If you find this is true, work on those issues, no matter how difficult they may seem at first; resolving them will help you greatly in the long run.

One of the best ways to practice this is by learning to say no. To do so effectively, first make sure you genuinely feel that a request or a problem is not your concern. If you feel that it is not:

- Say no politely but firmly. Showing anger or irritation will only weaken your position and make the other person asking for something angry in return—not a good working situation.
- Show some sympathy to the request. Usually the request will have some validity. Acknowledge this.
- State your reasons for saying no. Backing yourself up with an explanation will convince the person that you are serious and will prevent any ill will.
- Never play a power game. If you're saying no just to prove a point or show someone how much power you have, you are asking for trouble. Not only are you creating a bad working environment, if you ever need

a favor, don't come to that person—they will not be
kindly disposed to help.

- Make sure you have the authority to say no. If the
  person can then go over your head, you will lose
  credibility. If there is any question that you may be
  overruled, say so. Spell out your own reasons for saying
  no, leaving the door open for the opposite outcome.